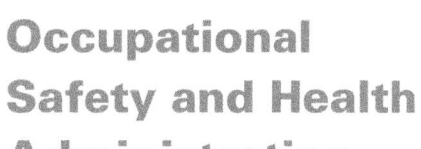

www.osha.gov

I0494226

Small Business Handbook

Small Business Safety and
Health Management Series

OSHA 2209-02R 2005

Employers are responsible for providing a safe and healthy workplace for their employees. OSHA's role is to promote the safety and health of America's working men and women by setting and enforcing standards; providing training, outreach and education; establishing partnerships; and encouraging continual improvement in workplace safety and health.

About this Handbook

This handbook is provided to owners, proprietors and managers of small businesses by the Occupational Safety and Health Administration (OSHA), an agency of the U.S. Department of Labor. For additional copies of this publication, write to the U.S. Government Printing Office, (GPO), Superintendent of Documents, Mail Stop SDE, 732 N. Capitol Street, NW, Washington, DC 20401, or call the OSHA Publications Office at (202) 693-1888, or fax (202) 693-2498 for ordering information. Please note that the entire text of the Small Business Handbook is available on OSHA's website at http://www.osha.gov/Publications/osha2209.pdf.

The handbook should help small business employers meet the legal requirements imposed by the *Occupational Safety and Health Act of 1970* (the Act), and achieve an in-compliance status before an OSHA inspection. An excellent resource to accompany this information is OSHA's Safety and Health Program Management Guidelines, (54 *Federal Register* 3904-3916, January 26, 1989), also available on OSHA's website.

This handbook is not a legal interpretation of the provisions of the Act and does not place any additional requirements on employers or employees.

Employers cannot be cited under the General Duty Clause in Section 5(a)(1) of the Act for failure to follow recommendations in this handbook.

The materials in this handbook are based upon Federal OSHA standards and other requirements in effect at the time of publication and upon generally accepted principles and activities within the job safety and health field. They should be useful to small business owners or managers and can be adapted easily to individual establishments.

It is important to point out that 24 states, Puerto Rico and the Virgin Islands operate their own OSHA-approved safety and health programs under Section 18 of the Act. While the programs in these State Plan States may differ in some respects from Federal OSHA, this handbook can be used by employers in any state because the standards imposed by State Plan States must be at least as effective as Federal OSHA standards. A list of states that operate their own safety and health programs can be found on OSHA's website at www.osha.gov.

Material in this publication is in the public domain and may be reproduced, fully or partially, without permission. Source credit is requested but not required.

This information will be made available to sensory impaired individuals upon request by voice phone (202) 693-1999 or teletypewriter (TTY) (877) 889-5627.

Please Note: The small business employer seeking information on procurement or contracting with the Department of Labor or OSHA should contact the Department of Labor's Office of Small Business Programs, 200 Constitution Avenue, NW, Room C-2318, Washington, DC 20210.

Small Business Handbook

Occupational Safety and Health Administration
U.S. Department of Labor

OSHA 2209-02R
2005

**Occupational Safety
and Health Administration**
U.S. Department of Labor
www.osha.gov

Contents

American employers and workers want safe and healthful places in which to work. They want everyone on the job to go home whole and healthy each day. Determined to make that dream possible, OSHA is committed to assuring – so far as possible – that every working man and woman in the nation has safe and healthful working conditions. OSHA believes that providing workers with a safe workplace is central to their ability to enjoy health, security and the opportunity to achieve the American dream.

OSHA seeks to cut unnecessary rules, regulations and red tape. It is eliminating thousands of pages of outdated regulations and continues to rewrite standards in plain English. OSHA is paring down its regulatory agenda so that it more accurately reflects realistic goals that best serve the needs of American employers and employees.

Confronted by the realities and demands to keep pace with the workforce and problems of the future, OSHA is developing new strategies to reduce occupational fatalities, injuries and illnesses. Coupled with strong, effective and fair enforcement, OSHA strives to provide improved outreach, education and compliance assistance to America's employers and employees.

Office of Small Business Assistance

OSHA wants to provide quality service to our small business customers. In October 2002, OSHA created the Office of Small Business Assistance to provide small business direction, to facilitate information sharing and to help in finding and achieving regulatory compliance. The office also works to educate small businesses on using up-to-date tools and materials, and facilitates opportunities to comment on OSHA's regulatory agenda. The Office of Small Business Assistance maintains OSHA's specialized small business web pages found at http://www.osha.gov/dcsp/smallbusiness/index.html.

The Office of Small Business Assistance can be contacted by telephone at (202) 693-2220 or by writing to: Director, Office of Small Business Assistance, 200 Constitution Avenue, N.W., Room N-3700, Washington, DC 20210.

Cooperative Programs

Years of experience show us that voluntary collaborative relationships between OSHA, the private sector and other government entities lead to improved safety and health. As a result, OSHA continues to expand its cooperative programs which currently include the free and confidential Consultation Program, the Voluntary Protection Programs, the Strategic Partnership Program and OSHA's newest addition, Alliances. For a more detailed description of each of these programs, please see pages 40- 42.

Small businesses are encouraged to investigate the full array of cooperative programs offered by OSHA. Participation can be on an individual company basis or through an industry association. Detailed information on each program is also available on OSHA's website at www.osha.gov, by contacting any OSHA office, or by calling (800) 321-OSHA.

State Plans

OSHA has important partnerships with the 24 states, Puerto Rico and the Virgin Islands that operate their own OSHA-approved safety and health programs. State workplace safety and health programs frequently lead the way in developing innovative approaches to making America's workplaces safer and healthier.

States that operate their own worker safety and health plans must provide worker protection that is "at least as effective as" the Federal program. However, because their standards and other procedures may vary, businesses should become familiar with their state regulations and agencies. See OSHA's website for a list of State Plan States.

Office of Training and Education

OSHA's Office of Training and Education provides training and instruction in all facets of occupational safety and health. OSHA's Training Institute, located in Arlington Heights, IL, provides training for OSHA compliance safety and health officers as well as for the general public and safety and health staff from other Federal agencies. In addition to OSHA's Training Institute, there are 32 additional education sites located throughout the country. These OSHA education centers operate in conjunction with universities, colleges and learning centers to conduct OSHA courses for the private sector and other Federal agencies, making safety and health training and education more accessible to those who need it. There are tuition fees for private sector students. For more information about OSHA's Training Institute, OSHA's education centers, or to obtain training catalogs with course schedules, write the OSHA Training Institute, 2020 South Arlington Heights Road, Arlington Heights, IL 60005 or call (847) 297-4810. The information is also fully accessible on the Internet at www.osha.gov.

OSHA's Website

OSHA has made every effort to continuously expand and improve its website. OSHA's extensive website provides employers and employees with practical, easy-to-understand and up-to-date guidance on regulations, compliance assistance and learning how to identify and control hazards. Each OSHA cooperative program has individual web pages describing program elements and highlighting successes of the participants. Several pages are devoted to small business, technical links, news items, publication lists and an inventory of compliance assistance tools, including expert advisors and eTools. eTools are "stand-alone" interactive, web-based training tools on occupational safety and health topics. Regulations, standards, directives and interpretations relating to OSHA can be found as well. There is a Spanish version of the OSHA website, and many posters and some publications are also available in Spanish.

OSHA's web pages include MyOSHA, which allows users to create their own personalized OSHA web page with customized content and links. Quick Start is another tool on OSHA's Compliance Assistance web page that allows the user to identify many of the major OSHA requirements and guidance materials that apply to their individual workplaces or industry sectors.

Through its website, OSHA invites citizens to e-mail questions that can be routed to appropriate agency officials for response. Any communication conducted via the "Contact Us" link on the OSHA website is considered an informational exchange rather than an official communication with the Department of Labor. For an official response to a question or concern, inquiries should be submitted in writing.

If you would like to receive regular updates from OSHA about new programs, tools, best practices and other useful information, subscribe to the agency's e-news memo, QuickTakes. QuickTakes is issued twice monthly to subscribers and is always available online. You can subscribe to OSHA's QuickTakes at www.osha.gov.

Safety and Health Add Value

Addressing safety and health issues in the workplace saves the employer money and adds value to the business. Recent estimates place the business costs associated with occupational injuries at close to $170 billion–expenditures that come straight out of company profits.

When workers stay whole and healthy, the direct cost-savings to businesses include:
- lower workers' compensation insurance costs;
- reduced medical expenditures;
- smaller expenditures for return-to-work programs;
- fewer faulty products;
- lower costs for job accommodations for injured workers;
- less money spent for overtime benefits.

Safety and health also make big reductions in indirect costs, due to:
- increased productivity;
- higher quality products;
- increased morale;
- better labor/management relations;
- reduced turnover;
- better use of human resources.

Employees and their families benefit from safety and health because:
- their incomes are protected;
- their family lives are not hindered by injury;
- their stress is not increased.

Simply put, protecting people on the job is in everyone's best interest–our economy, our communities, our fellow workers and our families. Safety and health add value to businesses, workplaces and lives.

OSHA
Occupational Safety and
Health Administration

A Profit and Loss Statement

As a small business owner, you are, by nature, a risk taker. You wager your business acumen against larger, perhaps more heavily financed corporate groups and other free-spirited, self-employed individuals like yourself. There is excitement and challenge in such a venture, but to succeed you need good management information, an ability to be a good manager of people and the intelligence and inner strength to make the right decisions.

Thousands of workers die each year and many, many more suffer injury or illness from conditions at work. But how often does an owner or manager like you actually see or even hear about work-related deaths, serious injuries or illnesses in the businesses with which you are familiar? How often has your business actually sustained this type of loss?

In most small businesses, the answer is rarely. For this reason, many owners or managers do not understand why there is controversy about the Occupational Safety and Health Administration (OSHA), job safety and health standards, inspections, citations, etc.

But others have learned why. Unfortunately, they have experienced a loss. These owner/managers will tell you that it is too late to do anything once a serious accident happens. They have learned that **prevention** is the only real way to avoid this loss.

Reducing losses is a goal that you as an owner or manager share with us in OSHA. While we may see this goal in a slightly different light, it remains a common bond.

We have learned from small employers, like you, that you place a high value on the well-being of your employees. Like many small businesses, you may employ family members and personal acquaintances. And, if you don't know your employees before they are hired, then chances are that the very size of your workplace will promote the closeness and concern for one another that small businesses value.

Assuming that you are committed to safe and healthful work practices, OSHA wants to work with you to prevent all losses. We believe that, when you make job safety and health a real part of your everyday operations, you will not lose in the long run. Investing in safety and health activity now will better enable you to avoid possible losses in the future.

Developing a Profitable Strategy for Handling Occupational Safety and Health

Nobody wants accidents to happen in his or her business. A serious fire, a permanent injury, or the death of an employee or owner can cause the loss of profit or even an entire business. To prevent such losses, you don't have to turn your business upside down. You may not have to spend a lot of money, either. You do need to use good business sense and apply recognized prevention principles.

There are reasons why accidents happen. Something goes wrong somewhere. It may take some thought, and maybe the help of friends or other trained people, to figure out **what** went wrong, but an accident always has a cause–a reason why. Once you know why an accident happened, it is possible to prevent future incidents. You need some basic facts and perhaps some help from others who already know some of the answers. You also need a plan–a plan to prevent accidents.

Not all dangers at your worksite depend on an accident to cause harm, of course. Worker exposure to toxic chemicals or harmful levels of noise or radiation may happen in conjunction with **routine** work as well as by accident. You may not realize the extent of the exposure or harm that you and your employees face. The effect may not be immediate. You need a plan that includes prevention of these health hazard exposures and accidents. You need a *safety and health management system.*

It is not difficult to develop such a plan. Basically, your plan should address the types of accidents and health hazard exposures that *could* happen in your workplace. Because each workplace is different, your program should address your specific needs and requirements.

There are four basic elements to all good safety and health programs. These are as follows:

1. Management Commitment and Employee Involvement. The manager or management team leads the way, by setting policy, assigning and supporting responsibility, setting an example and involving employees.

2. Worksite Analysis. The worksite is continually analyzed to identify all existing and potential hazards.

3. Hazard Prevention and Control. Methods to prevent or control existing or potential hazards are put in place and maintained.

4. Training for Employees, Supervisors and Managers. Managers, supervisors and employees are trained to understand and deal with worksite hazards.

Regardless of the size of your business, you should use each of these elements to prevent workplace accidents and possible injuries and illnesses.

Developing a workplace program following these four points is a key step in protecting you and your workers' safety and health. If you already have a program, reviewing it in relation to these elements should help you improve what you have.

Following this four-point approach to safety and health in your business may also improve efficiency. It may help you reduce insurance claims and other costs. While having a safety and health plan based on these four elements does not guarantee compliance with OSHA standards, the approach will help you toward full compliance and beyond.

It will certainly give you a way to express and document your good faith and commitment to protecting your workers' health and safety.

This approach usually does not involve large costs. Developing a health and safety protection plan does not have to be expensive and generally does not require additional employees, especially in smaller businesses. Safety and health can be integrated into your other business functions with modest effort on your part.

The key to the success of a safety and health plan is to see it as a part of your business operation and to see it reflected in your day-to-day operations. As you implement the plan and incorporate it into your business culture, safety and health awareness will become second nature to you and your employees.

The next section provides short descriptions and illustrations of each element. Since most employers, like you, are pressed for time, these descriptions will assist you in getting started on your own approach.

The Four-Point Workplace Program described here is based upon the Safety and Health Program Management Guidelines issued by OSHA in January 1989. (For a free copy of the guidelines, go to OSHA's website at www.osha.gov, write to OSHA Publications, U.S. Department of Labor, P.O. Box 37535, Washington, DC 200013-7535, or call (202) 693-1888.) Although voluntary, these guidelines represent OSHA's policy on what every worksite should have in place to protect workers from occupational hazards. The guidelines are based heavily on OSHA's experience with its Voluntary Protection Programs (VPP), which recognize excellence in workplace safety and health management. For more information on these guidelines and OSHA's cooperative programs, contact OSHA's Office of Small Business Assistance, U.S. Department of Labor, 200 Constitution Avenue, NW, Room N-3700, Washington, DC 20210, (202) 693-2220.

Using the Four-Point Program

As you review this publication, we encourage you to use the Action Plan Worksheet in Appendix A to jot down the things you want to do to make your workplace safe for your employees. Noting those actions as you go along will make it easier to assemble the total plan you need.

MANAGEMENT COMMITMENT AND EMPLOYEE INVOLVEMENT

As the owner or manager of a small business, your attitude toward job safety and health will be reflected by your employees. If you are not interested in preventing employee injury and illness, your employees will probably not give safety and health much thought either.

Therefore, it is essential that you demonstrate at all times your personal concern for employee safety and health, and the priority you place on them in your workplace. Your policy must be clear. Only you can show its importance through your own actions.

You can demonstrate the depth of your commitment by involving your employees in planning and carrying out your efforts. If you seriously involve your employees in identifying and resolving safety and health problems, they will bring their unique insights and energy to achieving the goals and objectives of your program. The men and women who work for you are among the most valuable

assets you have. Their safety, health and goodwill are essential to the success of your business. Having them cooperate with you in protecting their safety and health not only helps to keep them healthy–it makes your job easier.

Here are some actions to consider:

- Post your policy on worker safety and health next to the Job Safety and Health Protection Poster where all employees can see it. (See Appendix B, Model Policy Statements.)

- Hold a meeting with all employees to communicate your safety and health policy, and discuss your objectives for safety and health.

- Make sure that your support is visible by getting personally involved in the activities that are part of your safety and health program. For example, personally review all inspection and accident reports and ensure that follow-up occurs when needed.

- Ensure that you, your managers and your supervisors follow all safety requirements that apply to all employees, even if you are only in an area briefly. If, for instance, you require a hard hat, safety glasses and/or safety shoes in an area, wear them yourself when you are in that area.

- Take advantage of your employees' specialized knowledge and encourage them to buy into the program by having them make inspections, conduct safety training, or investigate accidents.

- Make clear assignments of responsibility for every part of your safety and health program, and make sure everyone understands them. The more people who are involved, the better. A good rule of thumb is to assign safety and health responsibilities in the same way you assign production responsibilities. Make it a special part of everyone's job to work safely.

- Give those with safety and health responsibility enough people, time, training, money and authority to get the job done.

- Don't forget your safety and health program

after you make assignments; make sure the job gets done. Recognize and reward those who do well and correct those who don't.

- At least once a year, review what you have accomplished in meeting your objectives and reevaluate whether you need new objectives or program revisions.

- Institute an accountability system where all personnel will be held accountable for not following work rules designed to promote workplace safety and health.

WORKSITE ANALYSIS

It is your responsibility to know what items or substances you have in your workplace that could hurt your workers. Worksite analysis is a group of processes that helps you make sure that you know what you need to keep your workers safe. For help in getting started with these processes, you can call on your state on-site Consultation Program and have an experienced health and safety professional visit your workplace for free and confidentially. Locations for each state are listed on OSHA's website. Also, OSHA's booklet, *Job Hazard Analysis,* may be helpful. (See OSHA Publications at page 42 for ordering information.)

Here are some actions to consider:

- Request a consultation visit from your state on-site Consultation Program covering both safety and health to get a full survey of the hazards that exist in your workplace and those that could develop. You can also contract for such services from expert private consultants if you prefer.

- Establish a way to get professional advice when you make changes to procedures or equipment, to ensure that the changes are not introducing new hazards into your workplace. Find ways to keep current on newly recognized hazards in your industry.

- Periodically review with employees each job, analyzing it step-by-step to see if there are any hidden hazards in the equipment or procedures.

- Set up a self-inspection system to check your hazard controls and evaluate any new haz-

ards. The checklists (at pages 18-39) provide a starting point. Your state consultant can assist you in establishing an effective system.

- Make sure your employees feel comfortable in alerting you or another member of management when they see things that look dangerous or out of place.

- Learn how to conduct a thorough investigation when things go wrong. This will help you develop ways to prevent recurrences. Extensive information can be found on OSHA's website under "Accident Investigation" in the index.

- Review several years of injury or illness records to identify patterns that can help you devise strategies to improve your safety and health program. Periodically review several months of experience to determine if any new patterns are developing.

HAZARD PREVENTION AND CONTROL

Once you have identified your existing and potential hazards, you are ready to implement the systems that prevent or control those hazards. Your state Consultation Program can help you do this. Whenever possible, hazards should be eliminated. Sometimes that can be done through substitution of a less toxic material or engineering controls. When you cannot eliminate hazards, systems should be established to control them.

Here are some actions to consider:

- Set up safe work procedures based on an analysis of the hazards in your workplace and ensure that employees understand and follow them. It is a good idea to involve employees in the analysis that results in those procedures. (See Appendix C, Codes of Safe Practices.)

- Be ready to enforce the rules for safe work procedures. Ask your employees to help you establish a disciplinary system that will be fair and understood by everyone.

- Where necessary, ensure that personal protective equipment (PPE) is used and that your employees know why they need it, how to use it and how to maintain it.

- Provide for regular equipment maintenance to prevent breakdowns that can create hazards. Ensure that preventive and regular maintenance are tracked to completion.

- Plan for emergencies, including fire and natural disasters. Conduct frequent drills to ensure that all employees know what to do under stressful conditions.

- Ask your state consultant to help develop a medical program that fits your worksite. Involve nearby doctors and emergency facilities by inviting them to visit your workplace and help you plan the best way to avoid injuries and illness during emergency situations.

- Ensure the ready availability of medical personnel for advice and consultation on matters of employee health. **This does not mean that you must provide health care,** but you must be prepared to deal with medical emergencies or health problems connected to your workplace.

To fulfill the above requirements, consider the following:

- Develop an emergency medical procedure to handle injuries, transport ill or injured workers and notify medical facilities. Posting emergency numbers is a good idea.

- Survey the medical facilities near your place of business and make arrangements for them to handle routine and emergency cases. Cooperative agreements may be possible with nearby larger workplaces that have on-site medical personnel and/or facilities.

- Ensure that your procedure for reporting injuries and illnesses is understood by all employees.

- Perform routine walkthroughs of the worksite to identify hazards and to track identified hazards until they are corrected.

- If your business is remote from medical facilities, you are **required** to ensure that adequately trained personnel are available to render first aid. First-aid supplies must be readily available for emergency use. Arrangements for this training can be made through your local Red Cross chapter, your insurance carrier, your local safety council, and others.

- Check battery charging stations, maintenance operations, laboratories, heating and ventilating operations and any corrosive materials areas to make sure the **required** eyewash facilities and showers are operational.

- Consider retaining a local doctor or an occupational health nurse on a part-time or as-needed basis for advice on medical and first aid planning.

TRAINING FOR EMPLOYEES, SUPERVISORS AND MANAGERS

An effective accident prevention program requires proper job performance from everyone in the workplace.

As an owner or manager, you must ensure that all employees know about the materials and equipment they work with, known hazards and how to control the hazards.

Each employee needs to know that:
- no employee is expected to undertake a job until he or she has received job instructions on how to do it properly and is authorized to perform that job. Also,
- no employee should undertake a job that appears unsafe.

You may be able to combine safety and health training with other training, depending upon the types of hazards in your workplace.

Here are some actions to consider:

- Ask your state consultant to recommend training for your worksite. The consultant may be able to conduct training while he or she is there.

- Make sure you have trained your employees on every potential hazard that they could be exposed to and how to protect themselves. Then verify that they really understand what you taught them.

- Pay particular attention to your new employees and to employees who are moving to new jobs. Because they are learning new operations, they are more likely to get hurt.

- Train your supervisors to understand all the hazards faced by the employees and how to reinforce training with quick reminders and refreshers, or with disciplinary action if necessary.

- Make sure that your top management staff understand their safety and health responsibilities and how to hold subordinate supervisory employees accountable for theirs.

Documenting Your Activities

Document your activities in all elements of the Four-Point Workplace Program. Essential records, including those legally required for workers' compensation, insurance audits and government inspections must be maintained as long as the actual need exists or as required by law. Keeping records of your activities, such as policy statements, training sessions, safety and health meetings, information distributed to employees, and medical arrangements made, is greatly encouraged. Maintaining essential records also will demonstrate sound business management as supporting proof for credit applications, for showing "good faith" in reducing any proposed penalties from OSHA inspections, for insurance and other audits, and aid efficient review of your current safety and health activities for better control of your operations and to plan improvements.

Safety and Health Recordkeeping

Records of sales, costs, profits and losses are essential to all successful businesses. They enable the owner or manager to learn from experience and to make corrections for future operations. Records of accidents, related injuries, illnesses and property losses can serve the same purpose, if they are used in the same way. The primary purpose of OSHA-required recordkeeping is to retain information about accidents that have happened to help determine the causes and develop procedures to prevent a recurrence.

INJURY/ILLNESS RECORDS

OSHA rules for recording and reporting occupational injuries and illnesses affect 1.4 million establishments. Small businesses with 10 or fewer employees throughout the year are exempt from most of the requirements of the OSHA recordkeeping rules, as are a number of specific industries in the retail, service, finance, insurance and real estate sectors that are classified as low-hazard. Detailed information about OSHA recordkeeping rules can be found at http://www.osha.gov/recordkeeping/index.html or refer to 29 Code of Federal Regulations (CFR) 1904 for the specific exceptions.

OSHA recordkeeping can help the small business employer evaluate the success of safety and health activities. Success can be measured by a reduction or elimination of employee injuries and illnesses during a calendar year.

The OSHA recordkeeping system has five steps:

1. Obtain a report on every injury or job-related illness requiring medical treatment (other than basic first aid).

2. Record each injury or job-related illness on OSHA Form 300 (*Log of Work-Related Injuries and Illnesses*) using the instructions provided.

3. Prepare a supplementary record of occupational injuries and illnesses for recordable cases on OSHA Form 301 (Injury and Illness Incident Report).

4. Every year, prepare an annual summary using OSHA Form 300A (*Summary of Work-Related Injuries and Illnesses*). Post it no later than February 1, and keep it posted until May 1. A good place to post it is next to the OSHA Workplace Poster.

5. Retain these records for at least five years.

Periodically review these records to look for any patterns or repeat situations. These records can help you to identify high-risk areas that require your immediate attention.

Basic OSHA recordkeeping requirements address only injuries and illnesses, so you might consider expanding your own records to include all

incidents, including those where no injury or illness resulted. This information may assist you in pin-pointing unsafe conditions and/or procedures. Safety councils, insurance carriers and others can assist you in instituting such a system.

The employer is required to report to OSHA within eight hours of the accident, all work-related fatalities or multiple hospitalizations that involve three or more employees.

Even if your business is exempt from routine recordkeeping requirements, you may be selected by the Federal Bureau of Labor Statistics (BLS) or a related state agency for inclusion in an annual sample survey. You will receive a letter directly from the agency with instructions, if you are selected.

EXPOSURE RECORDS AND OTHERS

In addition to injury/illness records, certain OSHA standards require records on the exposure of employees to toxic substances and hazardous exposures, physical examination reports and employment records.

As you identify hazards, you will be able to determine whether these requirements apply to your workplace. Your records should be used in conjunction with your control procedures and with your self-inspection activity. They should not be considered merely as bookkeeping.

You can use this handbook to create a basic plan of action for starting a safety and health management system at your business. The action plan described in this section provides the most direct route to getting yourself organized to complete the Four-Point Program outlined in the previous section.

Decide to Start Now

The time to start your safety and health management system is **now.** You have a better picture of what constitutes a good safety and health program. Now you can address the practical concerns of putting these elements together and coming up with a program to suit your workplace.

Hopefully, you have been taking notes for your action plan as you reviewed the preceding description of the Four-Point Program. You should now be ready to decide what you want to accomplish and to determine what steps are necessary to achieve your goals. Next you need to determine how and when each step will be done and who will do it.

Your plan should consider your company's immediate needs and provide for ongoing, long-lasting worker protection. Once your plan is designed, it is important to follow through and use it in the workplace. You will then have a program to anticipate, identify and eliminate conditions or practices that could result in injuries and illnesses.

If you have difficulty deciding where to begin, a phone call to your state Consultation Program will help get you started. A state consultant will survey your workplace for existing or potential hazards. Then, if you request it, he or she will determine what you need to make your safety and health program effective. The consultant will work with you to develop a plan for making these improvements and to keep your program effective.

Whether you choose to work with a consultant or to develop your program yourself, many publications are available from your state on-site Consultation Program or from OSHA that spell out in greater detail the steps you can take to create an effective safety and health program for your workplace. The rewards for your efforts will be an efficient and productive workplace with a low level of loss and injury.

Designating Responsibility

You **must** decide who in your company is the most appropriate person to manage your safety and health system. Who can ensure that the program will become an integral part of your business? In many cases it will be you, the owner. Sometimes it will be a plant manager or key supervisor. It could even be an engineer, personnel specialist, or other staff member.

Whoever you choose should be committed to workplace safety and health, have the time to develop and manage the program, and be willing to take on the responsibility and accountability that goes with operating an effective program. The individual will need your full cooperation and support, but the ultimate responsibility for safety and health in your workplace rests on you.

Ask for Help

Federal occupational safety and health law allows a state to develop and operate its own occupational safety and health program in place of the Federal OSHA program. It is possible that the regulatory aspect of the law (setting of mandatory minimum standards and conducting inspections of workplaces) is being operated by your state government as opposed to Federal OSHA.

One of the first things to learn is which branch of government, Federal or state, has current jurisdiction over your business. If you are not sure what agency is responsible for administering workplace safety and health in your state, contact the nearest OSHA Area Office to find out. (See www.osha.gov). You will need certain Federal OSHA publications (or comparable state publications) for use in your safety and health activities, such as:

- Job Safety and Health Protection - OSHA 3165. You must display the Federal or state OSHA poster in your workplace. This poster is also available in Spanish (*Job Safety and Health Protection* OSHA 3167).

- OSHA standards that apply to your business. You need to have a copy of all OSHA standards that apply to your type of business available for reference. (See Appendix D.)

Occupational Safety and Health Administration

Standards are the regulations that OSHA uses to inspect for compliance and should be the baseline for your inspections in determining what to do when hazards are identified. Most businesses fall under OSHA's General Industry Standards. If you are involved with construction or maritime operations, you will need the standards that apply to these classifications. (In states with state-run occupational safety and health programs, use the appropriate state standards.)

- Recordkeeping requirements and the necessary forms.

- *Occupational Safety and Health Act of 1970.* You may want a copy of this legislation for reference.

Organize the Workplace

Poor housekeeping can contribute to low morale and sloppy work. Most safety action programs start with an intensive cleanup campaign in all areas of the workplace.

Get rid of unecessary items; provide proper waste containers; store flammables properly; make sure exits are not blocked; mark aisles and passageways; provide adequate lighting, etc.

Get everyone involved and impress upon employees that you want to make your workplace safer, more healthful and more efficient.

Start Gathering Specific Facts About Your Situation

Before making changes in your safety and health operations, you should gather information about the current conditions and business practices that comprise your safety and health program. This information can help you identify problems and determine what is needed to solve them.

Your workplace assessment should be conducted by the person responsible for your safety and health management system and/or a professional safety and health consultant. The assessment consists of two major activities:

1. A comprehensive safety and health survey of your entire facility will identify any existing or potential safety and health hazards. This initial survey should focus on evaluating workplace conditions with respect to safety and health regulations and generally recognized safe and healthful work practices. It should include checking on the use of any hazardous materials, observing employee work habits and practices, and discussing safety and health problems with employees. See the Self-Inspection Checklists (at pages 18-39), to help you get a good start on creating this initial survey.

2. The second major activity is to assess your existing safety and health program and identify areas that work well and those that need improvement. You should gather as much information as you can that relates to safety and health management in your workplace. You should include the following in this review:

- **Safety and health activities.** Examine ongoing activities as well as those tried previously, company policy statements, rules (both work and safety), guidelines for proper work practices and procedures, and records of training programs.

- **Equipment.** List your major equipment, what it is used for and where it is located. Special attention should be given to inspection schedules, maintenance activities, and plant and office layouts.

- **Employee capabilities.** Make an alphabetical list of all employees, showing the date hired, their job descriptions, and experience and training.

- **Accident and injury/illness history.** Review first-aid cases and workers' compensation insurance payments and awards, and review your losses. Compare your insurance rate with others in your group. Give special attention to recurring accidents, types of injuries, etc.

After gathering facts, see if any major problem areas emerge such as interruptions in your normal operations, too many employees taking too much time off due to illness or injury, too many damaged products, etc. General help with this kind of problem identification can often be obtained from compensation carriers, local safety councils, trade associations, state agencies, major suppliers or similarly situated businesses in the same industry.

If you discover a major problem, see what can be done to solve it. Once a problem is identified, you can work on the corrective action or a plan to control the problem. Take immediate action and make a record of what you have done. Even if you find no major problems, don't stop there. Now it is time to develop a comprehensive safety and health program to avoid any major problems in the future.

Establish a Four-Point Safety and Health Program

The success of any workplace safety and health program depends on careful planning. This means that you must take the time to analyze what you want to accomplish and develop an action plan in order to attain your goals. From this standpoint, you can design a step-by-step process to take you from the idea stage to an effective safety and health management system.

The best way to create a safe and healthful workplace is to institute the Four-Point Program discussed at page 8 of this handbook.

Establish your **management commitment** and **involve your employees.** No safety and health program will work without this commitment and involvement. The first step is to designate a person to be responsible for your safety and health program.

Involve your employees as widely as possible from the beginning. They are most in contact with the potential and actual safety and health hazards at your worksite and will have constructive input on the development of your program. The ultimate success of your safety and health program will depend on their support.

Make sure your program assigns responsibility and accountability to all employees in your organization. A good safety and health program makes it clear that each and every employee, from you through the supervisory levels to the line worker, carries responsibility for his or her part of the program. Make safety and health duties clear and hold every individual accountable for his or her safety- and health-related duties.

Refer to the recommended actions to take in the Worksite Analysis paragraph at page 9. These will help start your program off on the right track. You will be building the foundation for a successful safety and health program.

Establish and regularly conduct a **worksite analysis.** A successful safety and health program depends on an accurate identification of all the hazards and potential hazards in your workplace. This is an ongoing process that includes routine self-inspections.

Create systems and procedures to **prevent and control hazards** identified through your worksite analysis. OSHA standards can be helpful because they address controls in order of effectiveness and preference. The hierarchy of controls is engineering, administrative, work practice and PPE. Whenever feasible, engineering, administrative or work practice controls should be instituted even if they do not eliminate the hazard or reduce exposure. Use of such controls in conjunction with PPE will help reduce the hazard or exposure to the lowest practical level. Where no standard exists, creative problem-solving and consultant resources may help you create effective controls. The basic formula for controlling workplace hazards, in order of preference, includes:

- **Eliminating the hazard** from the machine, the method, the material or the facility.

- **Abating the hazard** by limiting exposure or controlling it at its source.

- **Training personnel** to be aware of the hazard and to follow safe work procedures to avoid it.

- Prescribing **PPE** for protecting employees against the hazard and ensuring that they not only use it, but that they know how to use it correctly.

Establish and provide ongoing **training for employees, supervisors and managers** to ensure that everyone at your worksite can recognize hazards and how to control them.

These points are crucial to a safe and healthful workplace for you and your employees, making it more difficult for accidents to occur and for work-related health problems to develop.

Develop and Implement Your Action Plan

Developing an action plan to build a safety and health program around the four points can serve as a "road map" to take your program to where you

want it to be. An action plan tells you what has to be done, the logical order in which to do it, who is responsible and where you want to be when you finish. It describes problems and solutions, but is not ironclad. An action plan can and should be changed to correspond with changes in the workplace.

A good action plan has two parts:

1. A list of major changes or improvements to make your safety and health program effective. Each item should be prioritized, have a target date for completion and identify who is responsible for implementation.

2. A specific plan to implement each major change or improvement, including what you want to accomplish, the steps required, who will be assigned to do what and a schedule for completion.

A worksheet to help you design an overall action plan and describe specific action steps appears in Appendix A.

Once a plan is established, put it into action, beginning with the highest priority item. Ensure that it is realistic, manageable and addresses the steps you have planned for that item. A detailed description of the steps required will help you keep track of your progress. Keep in mind that you can work on more than one item at a time and that priorities may change as other needs are identified or as your company's resources change.

Open communication with your employees is crucial to the success of your efforts. Their cooperation depends on them understanding what the safety and health program is all about, why it is important to them and how it affects their work. The more you do to involve them in the changes you are making, the smoother your transition will be.

Putting your action plan into operation at your workplace will be a major step toward implementing an effective safety and health program.

Remember, a safety and health program is a plan put into practice. Keep your program on track by periodically checking its progress and by calling on a state consultant when you need assistance.

Any good management system requires periodic review. Take a careful look at each component of your safety and health program to determine what is working well and what changes are needed. Once again, a state consultant can assist you in this area. Any necessary improvements can be turned into new safety and health objectives for the coming year. Developing new action plans to implement these improvements will continue progress toward an effective safety and health program, reduce your safety and health risks, and increase efficiency and profit.

Remember that it is important to document your activities. The best way to evaluate the success of your safety and health program is to have documentation of what you have done, which provides guidance on how you can make it work even better.

Technical assistance may be available to you as a small business owner or manager through your insurance carrier; your fellow businesspeople; suppliers of your durable equipment and raw materials; the local safety council; and many local, state and Federal agencies, including the state on-site Consultation Programs and closest OSHA Area Office.

Establishing a quality safety and health management system will take time and involve some resources, but you should be pleased with the results. Employees will feel reassured because of your commitment to their safety and health on the job. You may save money through increased productivity and reduced workers' compensation insurance costs. You may gain increased respect in your community. The tangible and intangible rewards for a solid safety and health program far outweigh the cost of an accident, injury or workplace fatality.

The most widely accepted way to identify hazards is to conduct safety and health inspections because the only way to be certain of an actual situation is to look at it directly from time to time.

Begin a program of self-inspection in your own workplace. Self-inspection is essential if you are to know where probable hazards exist and whether they are under control.

This section includes checklists designed to assist you in self-inspection fact-finding. The checklists can give you some indication of where to begin taking action to make your business safer and more healthful for all of your employees.

These checklists are by no means all-inclusive and not all of the checklists will apply to your business. You might want to start by selecting the areas that are most critical to your business, then expanding your self-inspection checklists over time to fully cover all areas that pertain to your business. Remember that a checklist is a tool to help, not a definitive statement of what is mandatory. Use checklists only for guidance.

Don't spend time with items that have no application to your business. Make sure that each item is seen by you or your designee and leave nothing to memory or chance. Write down what you see or don't see and what you think you should do about it.

Add information from your completed checklists to injury information, employee information, and process and equipment information to build a foundation to help you determine what problems exist. Then, as you use the OSHA standards in your problem-solving process, it will be easier for you to determine the actions needed to solve these problems.

Once the hazards have been identified, institute the control procedures described at page 9 and establish your four-point safety and health program.

Self-Inspection Scope

Your self-inspections should cover safety and health issues in the following areas:

- **Processing, Receiving, Shipping and Storage** – equipment, job planning, layout, heights, floor loads, projection of materials, material handling and storage methods, training for material handling equipment.

- **Building and Grounds Conditions** – floors, walls, ceilings, exits, stairs, walkways, ramps, platforms, driveways, aisles.

- **Housekeeping Program** – waste disposal, tools, objects, materials, leakage and spillage, cleaning methods, schedules, work areas, remote areas, storage areas.

- **Electricity** – equipment, switches, breakers, fuses, switch-boxes, junctions, special fixtures, circuits, insulation, extensions, tools, motors, grounding, national electric code compliance.

- **Lighting** – type, intensity, controls, conditions, diffusion, location, glare and shadow control.

- **Heating and Ventilation** – type, effectiveness, temperature, humidity, controls, natural and artificial ventilation and exhausting.

- **Machinery** – points of operation, flywheels, gears, shafts, pulleys, key ways, belts, couplings, sprockets, chains, frames, controls, lighting for tools and equipment, brakes, exhausting, feeding, oiling, adjusting, maintenance, lockout/tagout, grounding, work space, location, purchasing standards.

- **Personnel** – training, including hazard identification training; experience; methods of checking machines before use; type of clothing; PPE; use of guards; tool storage; work practices; methods for cleaning, oiling, or adjusting machinery.

- **Hand and Power Tools** – purchasing standards, inspection, storage, repair, types, maintenance, grounding, use and handling.

- **Chemicals** – storage, handling, transportation, spills, disposals, amounts used, labeling, toxicity or other harmful effects, warning signs, supervision, training, protective clothing and equipment, hazard communication requirements.

- **Fire Prevention** – extinguishers, alarms, sprinklers, smoking rules, exits, personnel assigned, separation of flammable materials and dangerous operations, explosion-proof fix-

tures in hazardous locations, waste disposal and training of personnel.

- **Maintenance** – provide regular and preventive maintenance on all equipment used at the worksite, recording all work performed on the machinery and by training personnel on the proper care and servicing of the equipment.

- **PPE** – type, size, maintenance, repair, age, storage, assignment of responsibility, purchasing methods, standards observed, training in care and use, rules of use, method of assignment.

- **Transportation** – motor vehicle safety, seat belts, vehicle maintenance, safe driver programs.

- **First-Aid Program/Supplies** – medical care facilities locations, posted emergency phone numbers, accessible first-aid kits.

- **Evacuation Plan** – establish and practice procedures for an emergency evacuation, e.g., fire, chemical/biological incidents, bomb threat; include escape procedures and routes, critical plant operations, employee accounting following an evacuation, rescue and medical duties and ways to report emergencies.

Self-Inspection Checklists

These checklists are by no means all-inclusive. You should add to them or delete items that do not apply to your business; however, carefully consider each item and then make your decision. You should refer to OSHA standards for specific guidance that may apply to your work situation. (**Note:** These checklists are typical for general industry but not for construction or maritime industries.)

EMPLOYER POSTING

☐ Is the required OSHA Job Safety and Health Protection Poster displayed in a prominent location where all employees are likely to see it?

☐ Are emergency telephone numbers posted where they can be readily found in case of emergency?

☐ Where employees may be exposed to toxic substances or harmful physical agents, has appropriate information concerning employee access to medical and exposure records and Material Safety Data Sheets (MSDSs) been posted or otherwise made readily available to affected employees?

☐ Are signs concerning exit routes, room capacities, floor loading, biohazards, exposures to x-ray, microwave, or other harmful radiation or substances posted where appropriate?

☐ Is the Summary of Work-Related Injuries and Illnesses (OSHA Form 300A) posted during the months of February, March and April?

RECORDKEEPING

☐ Are occupational injuries or illnesses, except minor injuries requiring only first aid, recorded as required on the OSHA 300 log?

☐ Are employee medical records and records of employee exposure to hazardous substances or harmful physical agents up-to-date and in compliance with current OSHA standards?

☐ Are employee training records kept and accessible for review by employees, as required by OSHA standards?

☐ Have arrangements been made to retain records for the time period required for each specific type of record? (Some records must be maintained for at least 40 years.)

☐ Are operating permits and records up-to-date for items such as elevators, air pressure tanks, liquefied petroleum gas tanks, etc.?

SAFETY AND HEALTH PROGRAM

☐ Do you have an active safety and health program in operation that includes general safety and health program elements as well as the management of hazards specific to your worksite?

☐ Is one person clearly responsible for the safety and health program?

☐ Do you have a safety committee or group made up of management and labor representatives that meets regularly and reports in writing on its activities?

☐ Do you have a working procedure to handle in-house employee complaints regarding safety and health?

☐ Are your employees advised of efforts and accomplishments of the safety and health program made to ensure they will have a workplace that is safe and healthful?

☐ Have you considered incentives for employees or workgroups who excel in reducing workplace injury/illnesses?

MEDICAL SERVICES AND FIRST AID

☐ Is there a hospital, clinic, or infirmary for medical care near your workplace or is at least one employee on each shift currently qualified to render first aid?

☐ Have all employees who are expected to respond to medical emergencies as part of their job responsibilities received first aid training; had hepatitis B vaccination made available to them; had appropriate training on procedures to protect them from bloodborne pathogens, including universal precautions; and have available and understand how to use appropriate PPE to protect against exposure to bloodborne diseases?*

*Pursuant to an OSHA memorandum of July 1, 1992, employees who render first aid only as a collateral duty do not have to be offered pre-exposure hepatitis B vaccine only if the employer includes and implements the following requirements in his/her exposure control plan: (1) the employer must record all first aid incidents involving the presence of blood or other potentially infectious materials before the end of the work shift during which the first aid incident occurred; (2) the employer must comply with post-exposure evaluation, prophylaxis and follow-up requirements of the Bloodborne Pathogens standard with respect to "exposure incidents, " as defined by the standard; (3) the employer must train designated first aid providers about the reporting procedure; (4) the employer must offer to initiate the hepatitis B vaccination series within 24 hours to all unvaccinated first aid providers who have rendered assistance in any situation involving the presence of blood or other potentially infectious materials.

☐ If employees have had an exposure incident involving bloodborne pathogens, was an immediate post-exposure medical evaluation and follow-up provided?

☐ Are medical personnel readily available for advice and consultation on matters of employees' health?

☐ Are emergency phone numbers posted?

☐ Are fully supplied first aid kits easily accessible to each work area, periodically inspected and replenished as needed?

☐ Have first aid kits and supplies been approved by a physician, indicating that they are adequate for a particular area or operation?

☐ Is there an eye-wash station or sink available for quick drenching or flushing of the eyes and body in areas where corrosive liquids or materials are handled?

FIRE PROTECTION

☐ Is your local fire department familiar with your facility, its location and specific hazards?

☐ If you have a fire alarm system, is it certified as required and tested annually?

☐ If you have interior standpipes and valves, are they inspected regularly?

☐ If you have outside private fire hydrants, are they flushed at least once a year and on a routine preventive maintenance schedule?

☐ Are fire doors and shutters in good operating condition?

☐ Are fire doors and shutters unobstructed and protected against obstructions, including their counterweights?

☐ Are fire door and shutter fusible links in place?

☐ Are automatic sprinkler system water control valves, air and water pressure checked periodically as required?

☐ Is the maintenance of automatic sprinkler systems assigned to responsible persons or to a sprinkler contractor?

☐ Are sprinkler heads protected by metal guards if exposed to potential physical damage?

OSHA
Occupational Safety and
Health Administration

☐ Is proper clearance maintained below sprinkler heads?

☐ Are portable fire extinguishers provided in adequate number and type and mounted in readily accessible locations?

☐ Are fire extinguishers recharged regularly with this noted on the inspection tag?

☐ Are employees periodically instructed in the use of fire extinguishers and fire protection procedures?

PERSONAL PROTECTIVE EQUIPMENT AND CLOTHING

☐ Has the employer determined whether hazards that require the use of PPE (e.g., head, eye, face, hand, or foot protection) are present or are likely to be present?

☐ If hazards or the likelihood of hazards are found, are employers selecting appropriate and properly fitted PPE suitable for protection from these hazards and ensuring that affected employees use it?

☐ Have both the employer and the employees been trained on PPE procedures, i.e., what PPE is necessary for job tasks, when workers need it, and how to properly wear and adjust it?

☐ Are protective goggles or face shields provided and worn where there is any danger of flying particles or corrosive materials?

☐ Are approved safety glasses required to be worn at all times in areas where there is a risk of eye injuries such as punctures, abrasions, contusions, or burns?

☐ Are employees who wear corrective lenses (glasses or contacts) in workplaces with harmful exposures required to wear *only* approved safety glasses, protective goggles, or use other medically approved precautionary procedures?

☐ Are protective gloves, aprons, shields, or other means provided and required where employees could be cut or where there is reasonably anticipated exposure to corrosive liquids, chemicals, blood, or other potentially infectious materials? See the OSHA Bloodborne Pathogens standard, 29 CFR 1910.1030(b), for the definition of "other potentially infectious materials. "

☐ Are hard hats required, provided and worn where danger of falling objects exists?

☐ Are hard hats periodically inspected for damage to the shell and suspension system?

☐ Is appropriate foot protection required where there is the risk of foot injuries from hot, corrosive, or poisonous substances, falling objects, crushing, or penetrating actions?

☐ Are approved respirators provided when needed? (See 29 CFR 1910.134 for detailed information on respirators or check OSHA's website at www.osha.gov).

☐ Is all PPE maintained in a sanitary condition and ready for use?

☐ Are food or beverages consumed only in areas where there is no exposure to toxic material, blood, or other potentially infectious materials?

☐ Is protection against the effects of occupational noise provided when sound levels exceed those of the OSHA Noise standard?

☐ Are adequate work procedures, PPE and other equipment provided and used when cleaning up spilled hazardous materials?

☐ Are appropriate procedures in place to dispose of or decontaminate PPE contaminated with, or reasonably anticipated to be contaminated with, blood or other potentially infectious materials?

GENERAL WORK ENVIRONMENT

☐ Are all worksites clean, sanitary and orderly?

☐ Are work surfaces kept dry and appropriate means taken to assure the surfaces are slip-resistant?

☐ Are all spilled hazardous materials or liquids, including blood and other potentially infectious materials, cleaned up immediately and according to proper procedures?

☐ Is combustible scrap, debris and waste stored safely and removed from the worksite promptly?

☐ Is all regulated waste, as defined in the OSHA Bloodborne Pathogens standard (29 CFR 1910.1030), discarded according to Federal, state and local regulations?

☐ Are accumulations of combustible dust routinely removed from elevated surfaces including the overhead structure of buildings, etc.?

☐ Is combustible dust cleaned up with a vacuum system to prevent suspension of dust particles in the environment?

☐ Is metallic or conductive dust prevented from entering or accumulating on or around electrical enclosures or equipment?

☐ Are covered metal waste cans used for oily or paint-soaked waste?

☐ Are all oil and gas-fired devices equipped with flame failure controls to prevent flow of fuel if pilots or main burners are not working?

☐ Are paint spray booths, dip tanks, etc., cleaned regularly?

☐ Are the minimum number of toilets and washing facilities provided and maintained in a clean and sanitary fashion?

☐ Are all work areas adequately illuminated?

☐ Are pits and floor openings covered or otherwise guarded?

☐ Have all confined spaces been evaluated for compliance with 29 CFR 1910.146? (Permit-required confined spaces.)

WALKWAYS

☐ Are aisles and passageways kept clear and marked as appropriate?

☐ Are wet surfaces covered with non-slip materials?

☐ Are holes in the floor, sidewalk, or other walking surface repaired properly, covered, or otherwise made safe?

☐ Is there safe clearance for walking in aisles where motorized or mechanical handling equipment is operating?

☐ Are materials or equipment stored in such a way that sharp projections will not interfere with the walkway?

☐ Are spilled materials cleaned up immediately?

☐ Are changes of direction or elevations readily identifiable?

☐ Are aisles or walkways that pass near moving or operating machinery, welding operations, or similar operations arranged so employees will not be subjected to potential hazards?

☐ Is adequate headroom provided for the entire length of any aisle or walkway?

☐ Are standard guardrails provided wherever aisle or walkway surfaces are elevated more than 30 inches (76.20 centimeters) above any adjacent floor or the ground?

☐ Are bridges provided over conveyors and similar hazards?

FLOOR AND WALL OPENINGS

☐ Are floor openings guarded by a cover, a guardrail, or equivalent on all sides (except at stairways or ladder entrances)?

☐ Are toeboards installed around the edges of permanent floor openings where persons may pass below the opening?

☐ Are skylight screens able to withstand a load of at least 200 pounds (90.7 kilograms)?

☐ Is the glass in windows, doors, glass walls, etc., subject to possible human impact, of sufficient thickness and type for the condition of use?

☐ Are grates or similar type covers over floor openings such as floor drains designed to allow unimpeded foot traffic or rolling equipment?

☐ Are unused portions of service pits and pits not in use either covered or protected by guardrails or equivalent?

☐ Are manhole covers, trench covers and similar covers, and their supports designed to carry a truck rear axle load of at least 20,000 pounds (9,072 kilograms) when located in roadways and subject to vehicle traffic?

☐ Are floor or wall openings in fire-resistant construction provided with doors or covers compatible with the fire rating of the structure and

provided with a self-closing feature when appropriate?

STAIRS AND STAIRWAYS

☐ Do standard stair rails or handrails on all stairways have at least four risers?

☐ Are all stairways at least 22 inches (55.88 centimeters) wide?

☐ Do stairs have landing platforms not less than 30 inches (76.20 centimeters) in the direction of travel and extend 22 inches (55.88 centimeters) in width at every 12 feet (3.6576 meters) or less of vertical rise?

☐ Do stairs angle no more than 50 and no less than 30 degrees?

☐ Are stairs of hollow-pan type treads and landings filled to the top edge of the pan with solid material?

☐ Are step risers on stairs uniform from top to bottom?

☐ Are steps slip-resistant?

☐ Are stairway handrails located between 30 inches (76.20 centimeters) and 34 inches (86.36 centimeters) above the leading edge of stair treads?

☐ Do stairway handrails have at least 3 inches (7.62 centimeters) of clearance between the handrails and the wall or surface they are mounted on?

☐ Where doors or gates open directly on a stairway, is a platform provided so the swing of the door does not reduce the width of the platform to less than 21 inches (53.34 centimeters)?

☐ Are stairway handrails capable of withstanding a load of 200 pounds (90.7 kilograms), applied within 2 inches (5.08 centimeters) of the top edge in any downward or outward direction?

☐ Where stairs or stairways exit directly into any area where vehicles may be operated, are adequate barriers and warnings provided to prevent employees from stepping into the path of traffic?

☐ Do stairway landings have a dimension measured in the direction of travel at least equal to the width of the stairway?

☐ Is the vertical distance between stairway landings limited to 12 feet (3.6576 meters) or less?

ELEVATED SURFACES

☐ Are signs posted, when appropriate, showing the elevated surface load capacity?

☐ Are surfaces that are elevated more than 30 inches (76.20 centimeters) provided with standard guardrails?

☐ Are all elevated surfaces beneath which people or machinery could be exposed to falling objects provided with standard 4-inch (10.16-centimeter) toeboards?

☐ Is a permanent means of access and egress provided to elevated storage and work surfaces?

☐ Is required headroom provided where necessary?

☐ Is material on elevated surfaces piled, stacked, or racked in a manner to prevent it from tipping, falling, collapsing, rolling, or spreading?

☐ Are dock boards or bridge plates used when transferring materials between docks and trucks or railcars?

EXITING OR EGRESS - EVACUATION

☐ Are all exits marked with an exit sign and illuminated by a reliable light source?

☐ Are the directions to exits, when not immediately apparent, marked with visible signs?

☐ Are doors, passageways or stairways that are neither exits nor access to exits, but could be mistaken for exits, appropriately marked "NOT AN EXIT," "TO BASEMENT," "STOREROOM," etc.?

☐ Are exit signs labeled with the word "EXIT" in lettering at least 5 inches (12.70 centimeters) high and the stroke of the lettering at least I/2-inch (1.2700 centimeters) wide?

☐ Are exit doors side-hinged?

- [ ] Are all exits kept free of obstructions?
- [ ] Are at least two means of egress provided from elevated platforms, pits, or rooms where the absence of a second exit would increase the risk of injury from hot, poisonous, corrosive, suffocating, flammable, or explosive substances?
- [ ] Are there sufficient exits to permit prompt escape in case of emergency?
- [ ] Are special precautions taken to protect employees during construction and repair operations?
- [ ] Is the number of exits from each floor of a building and the number of exits from the building itself appropriate for the building occupancy load?
- [ ] Are exit stairways that are required to be separated from other parts of a building enclosed by at least 2-hour fire-resistive construction in buildings more than four stories in height, and not less than 1-hour fire-resistive construction elsewhere?
- [ ] Where ramps are used as part of required exiting from a building, is the ramp slope limited to 1 foot (0.3048 meter) vertical and 12 feet (3.6576 meters) horizontal?
- [ ] Where exiting will be through frameless glass doors, glass exit doors, storm doors, etc., are the doors fully tempered and meet the safety requirements for human impact?

EXIT DOORS

- [ ] Are doors that are required to serve as exits designed and constructed so that the path of exit travel is obvious and direct?
- [ ] Are windows that could be mistaken for exit doors made inaccessible by means of barriers or railings?
- [ ] Are exit doors able to be opened from the direction of exit travel without the use of a key or any special knowledge or effort when the building is occupied?
- [ ] Is a revolving, sliding, or overhead door prohibited from serving as a required exit door?

- [ ] Where panic hardware is installed on a required exit door, will it allow the door to open by applying a force of 15 pounds (6.80 kilograms) or less in the direction of the exit traffic?
- [ ] Are doors on cold storage rooms provided with an inside release mechanism that will release the latch and open the door even if the door is padlocked or otherwise locked on the outside?
- [ ] Where exit doors open directly onto any street, alley, or other area where vehicles may be operated, are adequate barriers and warnings provided to prevent employees from stepping into the path of traffic?
- [ ] Are doors that swing in both directions and are located between rooms where there is frequent traffic provided with viewing panels in each door?

PORTABLE LADDERS

- [ ] Are all ladders maintained in good condition, joints between steps and side rails tight, all hardware and fittings securely attached, and moveable parts operating freely without binding or undue play?
- [ ] Are non-slip safety feet provided on each metal or rung ladder, and are ladder rungs and steps free of grease and oil?
- [ ] Are employees prohibited from placing a ladder in front of doors opening toward the ladder unless the door is blocked open, locked, or guarded?
- [ ] Are employees prohibited from placing ladders on boxes, barrels, or other unstable bases to obtain additional height?
- [ ] Are employees required to face the ladder when ascending or descending?
- [ ] Are employees prohibited from using ladders that are broken, have missing steps, rungs, or cleats, broken side rails, or other faulty equipment?
- [ ] Are employees instructed not to use the top step of ordinary stepladders as a step?

OSHA
Occupational Safety and
Health Administration

☐ When portable rung ladders are used to gain access to elevated platforms, roofs, etc., does the ladder always extend at least 3 feet (0.9144 meters) above the elevated surface?

☐ Are employees required to secure the base of a portable rung or cleat type ladder to prevent slipping, or otherwise lash or hold it in place?

☐ Are portable metal ladders legibly marked with signs reading "CAUTION - Do Not Use Around Electrical Equipment" or equivalent wording?

☐ Are employees prohibited from using ladders as guys, braces, skids, gin poles, or for other than their intended purposes?

☐ Are employees instructed to only adjust extension ladders while standing at a base (not while standing on the ladder or from a position above the ladder)?

☐ Are metal ladders inspected for damage?

☐ Are the rungs of ladders uniformly spaced at 12 inches (30.48 centimeters) center to center?

HAND TOOLS AND EQUIPMENT

☐ Are all tools and equipment (both company and employee-owned) used at the workplace in good condition?

☐ Are hand tools, such as chisels, punches, etc., which develop mushroomed heads during use, reconditioned or replaced as necessary?

☐ Are broken or fractured handles on hammers, axes and similar equipment replaced promptly?

☐ Are worn or bent wrenches replaced?

☐ Are appropriate handles used on files and similar tools?

☐ Are employees aware of hazards caused by faulty or improperly used hand tools?

☐ Are appropriate safety glasses, face shields, etc., used while using hand tools or equipment that might produce flying materials or be subject to breakage?

☐ Are jacks checked periodically to ensure they are in good operating condition?

☐ Are tool handles wedged tightly into the heads of all tools?

☐ Are tool cutting edges kept sharp so the tool will move smoothly without binding or skipping?

☐ Are tools stored in a dry, secure location where they cannot be tampered with?

☐ Is eye and face protection used when driving hardened or tempered studs or nails?

PORTABLE (POWER OPERATED) TOOLS AND EQUIPMENT

☐ Are grinders, saws and similar equipment provided with appropriate safety guards?

☐ Are power tools used with proper shields, guards, or attachments, as recommended by the manufacturer?

☐ Are portable circular saws equipped with guards above and below the base shoe?

☐ Are circular saw guards checked to ensure that they are not wedged up, leaving the lower portion of the blade unguarded?

☐ Are rotating or moving parts of equipment guarded to prevent physical contact?

☐ Are all cord-connected, electrically operated tools and equipment effectively grounded or of the approved double insulated type?

☐ Are effective guards in place over belts, pulleys, chains and sprockets on equipment such as concrete mixers, air compressors, etc.?

☐ Are portable fans provided with full guards or screens having openings 1/2 inch (1.2700 centimeters) or less?

☐ Is hoisting equipment available and used for lifting heavy objects, and are hoist ratings and characteristics appropriate for the task?

☐ Are ground-fault circuit interrupters provided on all temporary electrical 15 and 20 ampere circuits used during periods of construction?

☐ Are pneumatic and hydraulic hoses on power-operated tools checked regularly for deterioration or damage?

ABRASIVE WHEEL EQUIPMENT GRINDERS

☐ Is the work rest used and kept adjusted to within 1/8 inch (0.3175 centimeter) of the wheel?

- [ ] Is the adjustable tongue on the top side of the grinder used and kept adjusted to within 1/4 inch (0.6350 centimeters) of the wheel?
- [ ] Do side guards cover the spindle, nut and flange and 75 percent of the wheel diameter?
- [ ] Are bench and pedestal grinders permanently mounted?
- [ ] Are goggles or face shields always worn when grinding?
- [ ] Is the maximum revolutions per minute (rpm) rating of each abrasive wheel compatible with the rpm rating of the grinder motor?
- [ ] Are fixed or permanently mounted grinders connected to their electrical supply system with metallic conduit or other permanent wiring method?
- [ ] Does each grinder have an individual on and off control switch?
- [ ] Is each electrically operated grinder effectively grounded?
- [ ] Are new abrasive wheels visually inspected and ring tested before they are mounted?
- [ ] Are dust collectors and powered exhausts provided on grinders used in operations that produce large amounts of dust?
- [ ] Are splash guards mounted on grinders that use coolant to prevent the coolant from reaching employees?
- [ ] Is cleanliness maintained around grinders?

POWDER-ACTUATED TOOLS

- [ ] Are employees who operate powder-actuated tools trained in their use and required to carry a valid operator's card?
- [ ] Is each powder-actuated tool stored in its own locked container when not being used?
- [ ] Is a sign at least 7 inches (17.78 centimeters) by 10 inches (25.40 centimeters) with bold face type reading "POWDER-ACTUATED TOOL IN USE" conspicuously posted when the tool is being used?
- [ ] Are powder-actuated tools left unloaded until they are ready to be used?

- [ ] Are powder-actuated tools inspected for obstructions or defects each day before use?
- [ ] Do powder-actuated tool operators have and use appropriate PPE such as hard hats, safety goggles, safety shoes and ear protectors?

MACHINE GUARDING

- [ ] Is there a training program to instruct employees on safe methods of machine operation?
- [ ] Is there adequate supervision to ensure that employees are following safe machine operating procedures?
- [ ] Is there a regular program of safety inspection of machinery and equipment?
- [ ] Is all machinery and equipment kept clean and properly maintained?
- [ ] Is sufficient clearance provided around and between machines to allow for safe operations, set up and servicing, material handling and waste removal?
- [ ] Is equipment and machinery securely placed and anchored to prevent tipping or other movement that could result in personal injury?
- [ ] Is there a power shut-off switch within reach of the operator's position at each machine?
- [ ] Can electric power to each machine be locked out for maintenance, repair, or security?
- [ ] Are the noncurrent-carrying metal parts of electrically operated machines bonded and grounded?
- [ ] Are foot-operated switches guarded or arranged to prevent accidental actuation by personnel or falling objects?
- [ ] Are manually operated valves and switches controlling the operation of equipment and machines clearly identified and readily accessible?
- [ ] Are all emergency stop buttons colored red?
- [ ] Are all pulleys and belts within 7 feet (2.1336 meters) of the floor or working level properly guarded?
- [ ] Are all moving chains and gears properly guarded?

OSHA
Occupational Safety and
Health Administration

☐ Are splash guards mounted on machines that use coolant to prevent the coolant from reaching employees?

☐ Are methods provided to protect the operator and other employees in the machine area from hazards created at the point of operation, ingoing nip points, rotating parts, flying chips and sparks?

☐ Are machine guards secure and arranged so they do not cause a hazard while in use?

☐ If special hand tools are used for placing and removing material, do they protect the operator's hands?

☐ Are revolving drums, barrels and containers guarded by an enclosure that is interlocked with the drive mechanism so that revolution cannot occur unless the guard enclosure is in place?

☐ Do arbors and mandrels have firm and secure bearings, and are they free from play?

☐ Are provisions made to prevent machines from automatically starting when power is restored after a power failure or shutdown?

☐ Are machines constructed so as to be free from excessive vibration when the largest size tool is mounted and run at full speed?

☐ If machinery is cleaned with compressed air, is air pressure controlled and PPE or other safeguards utilized to protect operators and other workers from eye and body injury?

☐ Are fan blades protected with a guard having openings no larger than I/2 inch (1.2700 centimeters) when operating within 7 feet (2.1336 meters) of the floor?

☐ Are saws used for ripping equipped with anti-kickback devices and spreaders?

☐ Are radial arm saws so arranged that the cutting head will gently return to the back of the table when released?

LOCKOUT/TAGOUT PROCEDURES

☐ Is all machinery or equipment capable of movement required to be de-energized or disengaged and blocked or locked out during cleaning, servicing, adjusting, or setting up operations?

☐ If the power disconnect for equipment does not also disconnect the electrical control circuit, are the appropriate electrical enclosures identified and is a means provided to ensure that the control circuit can also be disconnected and locked out?

☐ Is the locking out of control circuits instead of locking out main power disconnects prohibited?

☐ Are all equipment control valve handles provided with a means for locking out?

☐ Does the lockout procedure require that stored energy (mechanical, hydraulic, air, etc.) be released or blocked before equipment is locked out for repairs?

☐ Are appropriate employees provided with individually keyed personal safety locks?

☐ Are employees required to keep personal control of their key(s) while they have safety locks in use?

☐ Is it required that only the employee exposed to the hazard can place or remove the safety lock?

☐ Is it required that employees check the safety of the lockout by attempting a startup after making sure no one is exposed?

☐ Are employees instructed to always push the control circuit stop button prior to re-energizing the main power switch?

☐ Is there a means provided to identify any or all employees who are working on locked-out equipment by their locks or accompanying tags?

☐ Are a sufficient number of accident prevention signs or tags and safety padlocks provided for any reasonably foreseeable repair emergency?

☐ When machine operations, configuration, or size require an operator to leave the control station and part of the machine could move if accidentally activated, is the part required to be separately locked out or blocked?

☐ If equipment or lines cannot be shut down, locked out and tagged, is a safe job procedure established and rigidly followed?

WELDING, CUTTING AND BRAZING

☐ Are only authorized and trained personnel permitted to use welding, cutting, or brazing equipment?

☐ Does each operator have a copy of and follow the appropriate operating instructions?

☐ Are compressed gas cylinders regularly examined for obvious signs of defects, deep rusting, or leakage?

☐ Is care used in handling and storage of cylinders, safety valves, relief valves, etc., to prevent damage?

☐ Are precautions taken to prevent the mixture of air or oxygen with flammable gases, except at a burner or in a standard torch?

☐ Are only approved apparatuses (torches, regulators, pressure reducing valves, acetylene generators, manifolds) used?

☐ Are cylinders kept away from sources of heat and elevators, stairs, or gangways?

☐ Is it prohibited to use cylinders as rollers or supports?

☐ Are empty cylinders appropriately marked and their valves closed?

☐ Are signs posted reading "DANGER, NO SMOKING, MATCHES, OR OPEN LIGHTS, " or the equivalent?

☐ Are cylinders, cylinder valves, couplings, regulators, hoses and apparatuses kept free of oily or greasy substances?

☐ Is care taken not to drop or strike cylinders?

☐ Are regulators removed and valve-protection caps put in place before moving cylinders, unless they are secured on special trucks?

☐ Do cylinders without fixed wheels have keys, handles, or non-adjustable wrenches on stem valves when in service?

☐ Are liquefied gases stored and shipped valve-end up with valve covers in place?

☐ Are employees trained never to crack a fuel gas cylinder valve near sources of ignition?

☐ Before a regulator is removed, is the valve closed and gas released?

☐ Is red used to identify the acetylene (and other fuel-gas) hose, green for the oxygen hose and black for inert gas and air hoses?

☐ Are pressure-reducing regulators used only for the gas and pressures for which they are intended?

☐ Is open circuit (no-load) voltage of arc welding and cutting machines as low as possible and not in excess of the recommended limits?

☐ Under wet conditions, are automatic controls for reducing no-load voltage used?

☐ Is grounding of the machine frame and safety ground connections of portable machines checked periodically?

☐ Are electrodes removed from the holders when not in use?

☐ Is it required that electric power to the welder be shut off when no one is in attendance?

☐ Is suitable fire extinguishing equipment available for immediate use?

☐ Is the welder forbidden to coil or loop welding electrode cable around his body?

☐ Are wet machines thoroughly dried and tested before use?

☐ Are work and electrode lead cables frequently inspected for wear and damage, and replaced when needed?

☐ Are cable connectors adequately insulated?

☐ When the object to be welded cannot be moved and fire hazards cannot be removed, are shields used to confine heat, sparks and slag?

☐ Are fire watchers assigned when welding or cutting is performed in locations where a serious fire might develop?

☐ Are combustible floors kept wet, covered with damp sand, or protected by fire-resistant shields?

☐ Are personnel protected from possible electrical shock when floors are wet?

☐ Are precautions taken to protect combustibles on the other side of metal walls when welding is underway?

☐ Are used drums, barrels, tanks and other containers thoroughly cleaned of substances that could explode, ignite, or produce toxic vapors before hot work begins?

☐ Do eye protection, helmets, hand shields and goggles meet appropriate standards?

☐ Are employees exposed to the hazards created by welding, cutting, or brazing operations protected with PPE and clothing?

☐ Is a check made for adequate ventilation in and where welding or cutting is performed?

☐ When working in confined places, are environmental monitoring tests done and means provided for quick removal of welders in case of an emergency?

COMPRESSORS AND COMPRESSED AIR

☐ Are compressors equipped with pressure relief valves and pressure gauges?

☐ Are compressor air intakes installed and equipped so as to ensure that only clean, uncontaminated air enters the compressor?

☐ Are air filters installed on the compressor intake?

☐ Are compressors operated and lubricated in accordance with the manufacturer's recommendations?

☐ Are safety devices on compressed air systems checked frequently?

☐ Before a compressor's pressure system is repaired, is the pressure bled off and the system locked out?

☐ Are signs posted to warn of the automatic starting feature of the compressors?

☐ Is the belt drive system totally enclosed to provide protection for the front, back, top and sides?

☐ Are employees strictly prohibited from directing compressed air towards a person?

☐ Are employees prohibited from using highly compressed air for cleaning purposes?

☐ When compressed air is used to clean clothing, are employees trained to reduce the pressure to less than 10 pounds per square inch (psi)?

☐ When using compressed air for cleaning, do employees wear protective chip guarding and PPE?

☐ Are safety chains or other suitable locking devices used at couplings of high-pressure hose lines where a connection failure would create a hazard?

☐ Before compressed air is used to empty containers of liquid, is the safe working pressure of the container checked?

☐ When compressed air is used with abrasive blast cleaning equipment, is the operating valve a type that must be held open manually?

☐ When compressed air is used to inflate auto tires, are a clip-on chuck and an inline regulator preset to 40 psi required?

☐ Are employees prohibited from using compressed air to clean up or move combustible dust if such action could cause the dust to be suspended in the air and cause a fire or explosion hazard?

COMPRESSORS/AIR RECEIVERS

☐ Is every receiver equipped with a pressure gauge and one or more automatic, spring-loaded safety valves?

☐ Is the total relieving capacity of the safety valve able to prevent pressure in the receiver from exceeding the maximum allowable working pressure of the receiver by more than 10 percent?

☐ Is every air receiver provided with a drain pipe and valve at the lowest point for the removal of accumulated oil and water?

☐ Are compressed air receivers periodically drained of moisture and oil?

☐ Are all safety valves tested at regular intervals to determine whether they are in good operating condition?

☐ Is there a current operating permit?

☐ Is the inlet of air receivers and piping systems kept free of accumulated oil and carbonaceous materials?

COMPRESSED GAS CYLINDERS

- ☐ Are cylinders with a water weight capacity over 30 pounds (13.6 kilograms) equipped with a means to connect a valve protector device, or with a collar or recess to protect the valve?

- ☐ Are cylinders legibly marked to clearly identify the type of gas?

- ☐ Are compressed gas cylinders stored in areas protected from external heat sources such as flame impingement, intense radiant heat, electric arcs, or high-temperature lines?

- ☐ Are cylinders located or stored in areas where they will not be damaged by passing or falling objects or subject to tampering by unauthorized persons?

- ☐ Are cylinders stored or transported in a manner to prevent them from creating a hazard by tipping, falling, or rolling?

- ☐ Are cylinders containing liquefied fuel gas stored or transported in a position so that the safety relief device is always in direct contact with the vapor space in the cylinder?

- ☐ Are valve protectors always placed on cylinders when the cylinders are not in use or connected for use?

- ☐ Are all valves closed off before a cylinder is moved, when the cylinder is empty and at the completion of each job?

- ☐ Are low-pressure fuel gas cylinders checked periodically for corrosion, general distortion, cracks, or any other defect that might indicate a weakness or render them unfit for service?

- ☐ Does the periodic check of low-pressure fuel gas cylinders include a close inspection of the cylinders' bottoms?

HOIST AND AUXILIARY EQUIPMENT

- ☐ Is each overhead electric hoist equipped with a limit device to stop the hook at its highest and lowest point of safe travel?

- ☐ Will each hoist automatically stop and hold any load up to 125 percent of its rated load if its actuating force is removed?

- ☐ Is the rated load of each hoist legibly marked and visible to the operator?

- ☐ Are stops provided at the safe limits of travel for trolley hoists?

- ☐ Are the controls of hoists plainly marked to indicate the direction of travel or motion?

- ☐ Is each cage-controlled hoist equipped with an effective warning device?

- ☐ Are close-fitting guards or other suitable devices installed on each hoist to ensure that hoist ropes will be maintained in the sheave grooves?

- ☐ Are all hoist chains or ropes long enough to handle the full range of movement of the application while maintaining two full wraps around the drum at all times?

- ☐ Are guards provided for nip points or contact points between hoist ropes and sheaves permanently located within 7 feet (2.1336 meters) of the floor, ground, or working platform?

- ☐ Are employees prohibited from using chains or rope slings that are kinked or twisted and prohibited from using the hoist rope or chain wrapped around the load as a substitute for a sling?

- ☐ Is the operator instructed to avoid carrying loads above people?

INDUSTRIAL TRUCKS - FORKLIFTS

- ☐ Are employees properly trained in the use of the type of industrial truck they operate?

- ☐ Are only trained personnel allowed to operate industrial trucks?

- ☐ Is substantial overhead protective equipment provided on high lift rider equipment?

- ☐ Are the required lift truck operating rules posted and enforced?

- ☐ Is directional lighting provided on each industrial truck that operates in an area with less than 2 footcandles per square foot of general lighting?

- ☐ Does each industrial truck have a warning horn, whistle, gong, or other device that can be clearly heard above normal noise in the areas where it is operated?

**Occupational Safety and
Health Administration**

☐ Are the brakes on each industrial truck capable of bringing the vehicle to a complete and safe stop when fully loaded?

☐ Does the parking brake of the industrial truck prevent the vehicle from moving when unattended?

☐ Are industrial trucks that operate where flammable gases, vapors, combustible dust, or ignitable fibers may be present approved for such locations?

☐ Are motorized hand and hand/rider trucks designed so that the brakes are applied and power to the drive motor shuts off when the operator releases his or her grip on the device that controls the truck's travel?

☐ Are industrial trucks with internal combustion engines that are operated in buildings or enclosed areas carefully checked to ensure that such operations do not cause harmful concentrations of dangerous gases or fumes?

☐ Are safe distances maintained from the edges of elevated ramps and platforms?

☐ Are employees prohibited from standing or passing under elevated portions of trucks, whether loaded or empty?

☐ Are unauthorized employees prohibited from riding on trucks?

☐ Are operators prohibited from driving up to anyone standing in front of a fixed object?

☐ Are arms and legs kept inside the running lines of the truck?

☐ Are loads handled only within the rated capacity of the truck?

☐ Are trucks in need of repair removed from service immediately?

SPRAYING OPERATIONS

☐ Is adequate ventilation provided before spraying operations are started?

☐ Is mechanical ventilation provided when spraying operations are performed in enclosed areas?

☐ When mechanical ventilation is provided during spraying operations, is it so arranged that it will not circulate the contaminated air?

☐ Is the spray area free of hot surfaces and at least 20 feet (6.096 meters) from flames, sparks, operating electrical motors and other ignition sources?

☐ Are portable lamps used to illuminate spray areas suitable for use in a hazardous location?

☐ Is approved respiratory equipment provided and used when appropriate during spraying operations?

☐ Do solvents used for cleaning have a flash point to 100 degrees Fahrenheit (deg. F) or more?

☐ Are fire control sprinkler heads kept clean?

☐ Are "NO SMOKING" signs posted in spray areas, paint rooms, paint booths and paint storage areas?

☐ Is the spray area kept clean of combustible residue?

☐ Are spray booths constructed of metal, masonry, or other substantial noncombustible material?

☐ Are spray booth floors and baffles noncombustible and easily cleaned?

☐ Is infrared drying apparatus kept out of the spray area during spraying operations and is the spray booth completely ventilated before using the drying apparatus?

☐ Is the electric drying apparatus properly grounded?

☐ Are lighting fixtures for spray booths located outside the booth with the interior lighted through sealed clear panels?

☐ Are the electric motors for exhaust fans placed outside booths or ducts?

☐ Are belts and pulleys inside the booth fully enclosed?

☐ Do ducts have access doors to allow cleaning?

☐ Do all drying spaces have adequate ventilation?

ENTERING CONFINED SPACES

☐ Are confined spaces thoroughly emptied of any corrosive or hazardous substances, such as acids or caustics, before entry?

☐ Are all lines to a confined space that contain inert, toxic, flammable, or corrosive materials valved off and blanked or disconnected and separated before entry?

☐ Are all impellers, agitators, or other moving parts and equipment inside confined spaces locked out if they present a hazard?

☐ Is either natural or mechanical ventilation provided prior to confined space entry?

☐ Are appropriate atmospheric tests performed to check for oxygen deficiency, toxic substances and explosive concentrations in the confined space before entry?

☐ Is adequate illumination provided for the work to be performed in the confined space?

☐ Is the atmosphere inside the confined space frequently tested or continuously monitored during work?

☐ Is there a trained and equipped standby employee positioned outside the confined space, whose sole responsibility is to watch the work in progress, sound an alarm if necessary and render assistance?

☐ Is the standby employee appropriately trained and equipped to handle an emergency?

☐ Are employees prohibited from entering the confined space without lifelines and respiratory equipment if there is any question as to the cause of an emergency?

☐ Is approved respiratory equipment required if the atmosphere inside the confined space cannot be made acceptable?

☐ Is all portable electrical equipment used inside confined spaces either grounded and insulated or equipped with ground fault protection?

☐ Are compressed gas bottles forbidden inside the confined space?

☐ Before gas welding or burning is started in a confined space, are hoses checked for leaks, torches lighted only outside the confined area and the confined area tested for an explosive atmosphere each time before a lighted torch is taken into the confined space?

☐ If employees will be using oxygen-consuming equipment such as salamanders, torches, furnaces, etc., in a confined space, is sufficient air provided to assure combustion without reducing the oxygen concentration of the atmosphere below 19.5 percent by volume?

☐ Whenever combustion-type equipment is used in a confined space, are provisions made to ensure the exhaust gases are vented outside of the enclosure?

☐ Is each confined space checked for decaying vegetation or animal matter which may produce methane?

☐ Is the confined space checked for possible industrial waste which could contain toxic properties?

☐ If the confined space is below ground and near areas where motor vehicles will be operating, is it possible for vehicle exhaust or carbon monoxide to enter the space?

ENVIRONMENTAL CONTROLS

☐ Are all work areas properly illuminated?

☐ Are employees instructed in proper first aid and other emergency procedures?

☐ Are hazardous substances, blood and other potentially infectious materials, which may cause harm by inhalation, ingestion, or skin absorption or contact, identified?

☐ Are employees aware of the hazards involved with the various chemicals they may be exposed to in their work environment, such as ammonia, chlorine, epoxies, caustics, etc.?

☐ Is employee exposure to chemicals in the workplace kept within acceptable levels?

☐ Can a less harmful method or product be used?

☐ Is the work area ventilation system appropriate for the work performed?

☐ Are spray painting operations performed in spray rooms or booths equipped with an appropriate exhaust system?

☐ Is employee exposure to welding fumes controlled by ventilation, use of respirators, exposure time limits, or other means?

- [ ] Are welders and other nearby workers provided with flash shields during welding operations?

- [ ] If forklifts and other vehicles are used in buildings or other enclosed areas, are the carbon monoxide levels kept below maximum acceptable concentration?

- [ ] Has there been a determination that noise levels in the facilities are within acceptable levels?

- [ ] Are steps being taken to use engineering controls to reduce excessive noise levels?

- [ ] Are proper precautions being taken when handling asbestos and other fibrous materials?

- [ ] Are caution labels and signs used to warn of hazardous substances (e.g., asbestos) and biohazards (e.g., bloodborne pathogens)?

- [ ] Are wet methods used, when practicable, to prevent the emission of airborne asbestos fibers, silica dust and similar hazardous materials?

- [ ] Are engineering controls examined and maintained or replaced on a scheduled basis?

- [ ] Is vacuuming with appropriate equipment used whenever possible rather than blowing or sweeping dust?

- [ ] Are grinders, saws and other machines that produce respirable dusts vented to an industrial collector or central exhaust system?

- [ ] Are all local exhaust ventilation systems designed to provide sufficient air flow and volume for the application, and are ducts not plugged and belts not slipping?

- [ ] Is PPE provided, used and maintained wherever required?

- [ ] Are there written standard operating procedures for the selection and use of respirators where needed?

- [ ] Are restrooms and washrooms kept clean and sanitary?

- [ ] Is all water provided for drinking, washing and cooking potable?

- [ ] Are all outlets for water that is not suitable for drinking clearly identified?

- [ ] Are employees' physical capacities assessed before they are assigned to jobs requiring heavy work?

- [ ] Are employees instructed in the proper manner for lifting heavy objects?

- [ ] Where heat is a problem, have all fixed work areas been provided with spot cooling or air conditioning?

- [ ] Are employees screened before assignment to areas of high heat to determine if their health might make them more susceptible to having an adverse reaction?

- [ ] Are employees working on streets and roadways who are exposed to the hazards of traffic required to wear bright colored (traffic orange) warning vests?

- [ ] Are exhaust stacks and air intakes located so that nearby contaminated air will not be recirculated within a building or other enclosed area?

- [ ] Is equipment producing ultraviolet radiation properly shielded?

- [ ] Are universal precautions observed where occupational exposure to blood or other potentially infectious materials can occur and in all instances where differentiation of types of body fluids or potentially infectious materials is difficult or impossible?

FLAMMABLE AND COMBUSTIBLE MATERIALS

- [ ] Are combustible scrap, debris and waste materials (oily rags, etc.) stored in covered metal receptacles and promptly removed from the worksite?

- [ ] Is proper storage practiced to minimize the risk of fire, including spontaneous combustion?

- [ ] Are approved containers and tanks used to store and handle flammable and combustible liquids?

- [ ] Are all connections on drums and combustible liquid piping, vapor and liquid tight?

- [ ] Are all flammable liquids kept in closed containers when not in use (e.g., parts cleaning tanks, pans, etc.)?

- [ ] Are bulk drums of flammable liquids grounded and bonded to containers during dispensing?

- [ ] Do storage rooms for flammable and combustible liquids have explosion-proof lights and mechanical or gravity ventilation?

- [ ] Is liquefied petroleum gas stored, handled and used in accordance with safe practices and standards?

- [ ] Are "NO SMOKING" signs posted on liquefied petroleum gas tanks and in areas where flammable or combustible materials are used or stored?

- [ ] Are liquefied petroleum storage tanks guarded to prevent damage from vehicles?

- [ ] Are all solvent wastes and flammable liquids kept in fire-resistant, covered containers until they are removed from the worksite?

- [ ] Is vacuuming used whenever possible rather than blowing or sweeping combustible dust?

- [ ] Are firm separators placed between containers of combustibles or flammables that are stacked one upon another to ensure their support and stability?

- [ ] Are fuel gas cylinders and oxygen cylinders separated by distance and fire-resistant barriers while in storage?

- [ ] Are fire extinguishers selected and provided for the types of materials in the areas where they are to be used?

  Class A - Ordinary combustible material fires.

  Class B - Flammable liquid, gas or grease fires.

  Class C - Energized-electrical equipment fires.

- [ ] Are appropriate fire extinguishers mounted within 75 feet (22.86 meters) of outside areas containing flammable liquids and within 10 feet (3.048 meters) of any inside storage area for such materials?

- [ ] Are extinguishers free from obstructions or blockage?

- [ ] Are all extinguishers serviced, maintained and tagged at intervals not to exceed one year?

- [ ] Are all extinguishers fully charged and in their designated places?

- [ ] Where sprinkler systems are permanently installed, are the nozzle heads so directed or arranged that water will not be sprayed into operating electrical switchboards and equipment?

- [ ] Are safety cans used for dispensing flammable or combustible liquids at the point of use?

- [ ] Are all spills of flammable or combustible liquids cleaned up promptly?

- [ ] Are storage tanks adequately vented to prevent the development of excessive vacuum or pressure as a result of filling, emptying, or atmosphere temperature changes?

- [ ] Are storage tanks equipped with emergency venting that will relieve excessive internal pressure caused by fire exposure?

- [ ] Are rules enforced in areas involving storage and use of hazardous materials?

HAZARDOUS CHEMICAL EXPOSURE

- [ ] Are employees aware of the potential hazards and trained in safe handling practices for situations involving various chemicals stored or used in the workplace such as acids, bases, caustics, epoxies, phenols, etc.?

- [ ] Is employee exposure to chemicals kept within acceptable levels?

- [ ] Are eye-wash fountains and safety showers provided in areas where corrosive chemicals are handled?

- [ ] Are all containers, such as vats, storage tanks, etc., labeled as to their contents, e.g., "CAUSTICS"?

- [ ] Are all employees required to use personal protective clothing and equipment when handling chemicals (gloves, eye protection, respirators, etc.)?

- [ ] Are flammable or toxic chemicals kept in closed containers when not in use?

- [ ] Are chemical piping systems clearly marked as to their content?

- [ ] Where corrosive liquids are frequently handled in open containers or drawn from storage vessels or pipelines, are adequate means readily

OSHA
Occupational Safety and
Health Administration

available for neutralizing or disposing of spills or overflows and performed properly and safely?

☐ Are standard operating procedures established and are they being followed when cleaning up chemical spills?

☐ Are respirators stored in a convenient, clean and sanitary location, and are they adequate for emergencies?

☐ Are employees prohibited from eating in areas where hazardous chemicals are present?

☐ Is PPE used and maintained whenever necessary?

☐ Are there written standard operating procedures for the selection and use of respirators where needed?

☐ If you have a respirator protection program, are your employees instructed on the correct usage and limitations of the respirators? Are the respirators National Institute for Occupational Safety and Health (NIOSH)-approved for this particular application? Are they regularly inspected, cleaned, sanitized and maintained?

☐ If hazardous substances are used in your processes, do you have a medical or biological monitoring system in operation?

☐ Are you familiar with the threshold limit values or permissible exposure limits of airborne contaminants and physical agents used in your workplace?

☐ Have appropriate control procedures been instituted for hazardous materials, including safe handling practices and the use of respirators and ventilation systems?

☐ Whenever possible, are hazardous substances handled in properly designed and exhausted booths or similar locations?

☐ Do you use general dilution or local exhaust ventilation systems to control dusts, vapors, gases, fumes, smoke, solvents, or mists that may be generated in your workplace?

☐ Is operational ventilation equipment provided for removal of contaminants from production grinding, buffing, spray painting, and/or vapor degreasing?

☐ Do employees complain about dizziness, headaches, nausea, irritation, or other factors of discomfort when they use solvents or other chemicals?

☐ Is there a dermatitis problem? Do employees complain about dryness, irritation, or sensitization of the skin?

☐ Have you considered having an industrial hygienist or environmental health specialist evaluate your operation?

☐ If internal combustion engines are used, is carbon monoxide kept within acceptable levels?

☐ Is vacuuming used rather than blowing or sweeping dust whenever possible for cleanup?

☐ Are materials that give off toxic, asphyxiant, suffocating, or anesthetic fumes stored in remote or isolated locations when not in use?

HAZARDOUS SUBSTANCES COMMUNICATION

☐ Is there a list of hazardous substances used in your workplace and an MSDS readily available for each hazardous substance used?

☐ Is there a current written exposure control plan for occupational exposure to bloodborne pathogens and other potentially infectious materials, where applicable?

☐ Is there a written hazard communication program dealing with MSDSs, labeling and employee training?

☐ Is each container for a hazardous substance (i.e., vats, bottles, storage tanks, etc.) labeled with product identity and a hazard warning (communication of the specific health hazards and physical hazards)?

☐ Is there an employee training program for hazardous substances that includes:

- an explanation of what an MSDS is and how to use and obtain one;

- MSDS contents for each hazardous substance or class of substances;

- explanation of "A Right to Know";

- identification of where an employee can see

the written hazard communication program;

- location of physical and health hazards in particular work areas and the specific protective measures to be used; and

- details of the hazard communication program, including how to use the labeling system and MSDSs.

☐ Does the employee training program on the bloodborne pathogens standard contain the following elements:

- an accessible copy of the standard and an explanation of its contents;

- a general explanation of the epidemiology and symptoms of bloodborne diseases;

- an explanation of the modes of transmission of Bloodborne Pathogens;

- an explanation of the employer's exposure control plan and the means by which employees can obtain a copy of the written plan;

- an explanation of the appropriate methods for recognizing tasks and the other activities that may involve exposure to blood and other potentially infectious materials;

- an explanation of the use and limitations of methods that will prevent or reduce exposure, including appropriate engineering controls, work practices and PPE;

- information on the types, proper use, location, removal, handling, decontamination and disposal of PPE;

- an explanation of the basis for selection of PPE;

- information on the hepatitis B vaccine;

- information on the appropriate actions to take and persons to contact in an emergency involving blood or other potentially infectious materials;

- an explanation of the procedure to follow if an exposure incident occurs, including the methods of reporting the incident and the medical follow-up that will be made available;

- information on post-exposure evaluations and follow-up; and

- an explanation of signs, labels and color coding.

☐ Are employees trained in:

- how to recognize tasks that might result in occupational exposure;

- how to use work practice, engineering controls and PPE, and their limitations;

- how to obtain information on the types, selection, proper use, location, removal, handling, decontamination and disposal of PPE; and

- who to contact and what to do in an emergency.

ELECTRICAL

☐ Do you require compliance with OSHA standards for all contract electrical work?

☐ Are all employees required to report any obvious hazard to life or property in connection with electrical equipment or lines as soon as possible?

☐ Are employees instructed to make preliminary inspections and/or appropriate tests to determine conditions before starting work on electrical equipment or lines?

☐ When electrical equipment or lines are to be serviced, maintained, or adjusted, are necessary switches opened, locked out or tagged, whenever possible?

☐ Are portable electrical tools and equipment grounded or of the double insulated type?

☐ Are electrical appliances such as vacuum cleaners, polishers, vending machines, etc., grounded?

☐ Do extension cords have a grounding conductor?

☐ Are multiple plug adaptors prohibited?

☐ Are ground-fault circuit interrupters installed on each temporary 15 or 20 ampere, 120 volt alternating current (AC) circuit at locations where construction, demolition, modifications,

alterations, or excavations are being performed?

☐ Are all temporary circuits protected by suitable disconnecting switches or plug connectors at the junction with permanent wiring?

☐ Do you have electrical installations in hazardous dust or vapor areas? If so, do they meet the National Electrical Code (NEC) for hazardous locations?

☐ Are exposed wiring and cords with frayed or deteriorated insulation repaired or replaced promptly?

☐ Are flexible cords and cables free of splices or taps?

☐ Are clamps or other securing means provided on flexible cords or cables at plugs, receptacles, tools, equipment, etc., and is the cord jacket securely held in place?

☐ Are all cord, cable and raceway connections intact and secure?

☐ In wet or damp locations, are electrical tools and equipment appropriate for the use or location or otherwise protected?

☐ Is the location of electrical power lines and cables (overhead, underground, under floor, other side of walls, etc.) determined before digging, drilling, or similar work is begun?

☐ Are metal measuring tapes, ropes, hand-lines or similar devices with metallic thread woven into the fabric prohibited where they could come in contact with energized parts of equipment or circuit conductors?

☐ Is the use of metal ladders prohibited where the ladder or the person using the ladder could come in contact with energized parts of equipment, fixtures, or circuit conductors?

☐ Are all disconnecting switches and circuit breakers labeled to indicate their use or equipment served?

☐ Are disconnecting means always opened before fuses are replaced?

☐ Do all interior wiring systems include provisions for grounding metal parts of electrical raceways, equipment and enclosures?

☐ Are all electrical raceways and enclosures securely fastened in place?

☐ Are all energized parts of electrical circuits and equipment guarded against accidental contact by approved cabinets or enclosures?

☐ Is sufficient access and working space provided and maintained around all electrical equipment to permit ready and safe operations and maintenance?

☐ Are all unused openings (including conduit knockouts) in electrical enclosures and fittings closed with appropriate covers, plugs, or plates?

☐ Are electrical enclosures such as switches, receptacles, junction boxes, etc., provided with tight-fitting covers or plates?

☐ Are disconnecting switches for electrical motors in excess of two horsepower able to open the circuit when the motor is stalled without exploding? (Switches must be horsepower rated equal to or in excess of the motor rating.)

☐ Is low voltage protection provided in the control device of motors driving machines or equipment that could cause injury from inadvertent starting?

☐ Is each motor disconnecting switch or circuit breaker located within sight of the motor control device?

☐ Is each motor located within sight of its controller or is the controller disconnecting means able to be locked open or is a separate disconnecting means installed in the circuit within sight of the motor?

☐ Is the controller for each motor that exceeds two horsepower rated equal to or above the rating of the motor it serves?

☐ Are employees who regularly work on or around energized electrical equipment or lines instructed in cardiopulmonary resuscitation (CPR)?

☐ Are employees prohibited from working alone on energized lines or equipment over 600 volts?

NOISE

☐ Are there areas in the workplace where continuous noise levels exceed 85 decibels?

☐ Is there an ongoing preventive health program to educate employees in safe levels of noise, exposures, effects of noise on their health and the use of personal protection?

☐ Have work areas where noise levels make voice communication between employees difficult been identified and posted?

☐ Are noise levels measured with a sound level meter or an octave band analyzer and are records being kept?

☐ Have engineering controls been used to reduce excessive noise levels? Where engineering controls are determined to be infeasible, are administrative controls (i.e., worker rotation) being used to minimize individual employee exposure to noise?

☐ Is approved hearing protective equipment (noise attenuating devices) available to every employee working in noisy areas?

☐ Have you tried isolating noisy machinery from the rest of your operation?

☐ If you use ear protectors, are employees properly fitted and instructed in their use?

☐ Are employees in high noise areas given periodic audiometric testing to ensure that you have an effective hearing protection system?

FUELING

☐ Are employees prohibited from fueling an internal combustion engine with a flammable liquid while the engine is running?

☐ Are fueling operations performed to minimize spillage?

☐ When spillage occurs during fueling operations, is the spilled fuel washed away completely, evaporated, or are other measures taken to control vapors before restarting the engine?

☐ Are fuel tank caps replaced and secured before starting the engine?

☐ In fueling operations, is there always metal contact between the container and the fuel tank?

☐ Are fueling hoses designed to handle the specific type of fuel?

☐ Are employees prohibited from handling or transferring gasoline in open containers?

☐ Are open lights, open flames, sparking, or arcing equipment prohibited near fueling or transfer of fuel operations?

☐ Is smoking prohibited in the vicinity of fueling operations?

☐ Are fueling operations prohibited in buildings or other enclosed areas that are not specifically ventilated for this purpose?

☐ Where fueling or transfer of fuel is done through a gravity flow system, are the nozzles self-closing?

IDENTIFICATION OF PIPING SYSTEMS

☐ When nonpotable water is piped through a facility, are outlets or taps posted to alert employees that the water is unsafe and not to be used for drinking, washing, or other personal use?

☐ When hazardous substances are transported through above-ground piping, is each pipeline identified at points where confusion could introduce hazards to employees?

☐ When pipelines are identified by color painted bands or tapes, are the bands or tapes located at reasonable intervals and at each outlet, valve, or connection, and are all visible parts of the line so identified?

☐ When pipelines are identified by color, is the color code posted at all locations where confusion could introduce hazards to employees?

☐ When the contents of pipelines are identified by name or name abbreviation, is the information readily visible on the pipe near each valve or outlet?

☐ When pipelines carrying hazardous substances are identified by tags, are the tags constructed of durable materials, the message printed

OSHA
Occupational Safety and
Health Administration

clearly and permanently, and are tags installed at each valve or outlet?

When pipelines are heated by electricity, steam, or other external source, are suitable warning signs or tags placed at unions, valves, or other serviceable parts of the system?

MATERIALS HANDLING

Is there safe clearance for equipment through aisles and doorways?

Are aisleways permanently marked and kept clear to allow unhindered passage?

Are motorized vehicles and mechanized equipment inspected daily or prior to use?

Are vehicles shut off and brakes set prior to loading or unloading?

Are containers of liquid combustibles or flammables, when stacked while being moved, always protected by dunnage (packing material) sufficient to provide stability?

Are dock boards (bridge plates) used when loading or unloading operations are taking place between vehicles and docks?

Are trucks and trailers secured from movement during loading and unloading operations?

Are dock plates and loading ramps constructed and maintained with sufficient strength to support imposed loading?

Are hand trucks maintained in safe operating condition?

Are chutes equipped with sideboards of sufficient height to prevent the materials being handled from falling off?

Are chutes and gravity roller sections firmly placed or secured to prevent displacement?

Are provisions made to brake the movement of the handled materials at the delivery end of rollers or chutes?

Are pallets usually inspected before being loaded or moved?

Are safety latches and other devices being used to prevent slippage of materials off of hoisting hooks?

Are securing chains, ropes, chockers, or slings adequate for the job?

Are provisions made to ensure that no one is below when hoisting material or equipment?

Are MSDSs available to employees handling hazardous substances?

TRANSPORTING EMPLOYEES AND MATERIALS

Do employees who operate vehicles on public thoroughfares have valid operator's licenses?

When seven or more employees are regularly transported in a van, bus, or truck, is the operator's license appropriate for the class of vehicle being driven and are there enough seats?

Are vehicles used to transport employees equipped with lamps, brakes, horns, mirrors, windshields and turn signals, and are they in good repair?

Are transport vehicles provided with handrails, steps, stirrups, or similar devices, placed and arranged to allow employees to safely mount or dismount?

Are employee transport vehicles equipped at all times with at least two reflective-type flares?

Is a fully charged fire extinguisher, in good condition, with at least a 4 B:C rating maintained in each employee transport vehicle?

When cutting tools or tools with sharp edges are carried in passenger compartments of employee transport vehicles, are they placed in closed boxes or containers that are secured in place?

Are employees prohibited from riding on top of any load that could shift, topple, or otherwise become unstable?

CONTROL OF HARMFUL SUBSTANCES BY VENTILATION

Is the volume and velocity of air in each exhaust system sufficient to gather the dusts, fumes, mists, vapors, or gases to be controlled, and to convey them to a suitable point of disposal?

☐ Are exhaust inlets, ducts and plenums designed, constructed and supported to prevent collapse or failure of any part of the system?

☐ Are clean-out ports or doors provided at intervals not to exceed 12 feet (3.6576 meters) in all horizontal runs of exhaust ducts?

☐ Where two or more different operations are being controlled through the same exhaust system, could the combination of substances involved create a fire, explosion, or chemical reaction hazard in the duct?

☐ Is adequate makeup air provided to areas where exhaust systems are operating?

☐ Is the source point for makeup air located so that only clean, fresh air, free of contaminants will enter the work environment?

☐ Where two or more ventilation systems serve a work area, is their operation such that one will not offset the functions of the other?

SANITIZING EQUIPMENT AND CLOTHING

☐ Is required personal protective clothing or equipment able to be cleaned and disinfected easily?

☐ Are employees prohibited from interchanging personal protective clothing or equipment, unless it has been properly cleaned?

☐ Are machines and equipment that process, handle, or apply materials that could injure employees cleaned and/or decontaminated before being overhauled or placed in storage?

☐ Are employees prohibited from smoking or eating in any area where contaminants are present that could be injurious if ingested?

☐ When employees are required to change from street clothing into protective clothing, is a clean change room with a separate storage facility for street and protective clothing provided?

☐ Are employees required to shower and wash their hair as soon as possible after a known contact with a carcinogen has occurred?

☐ When equipment, materials, or other items are taken into or removed from a carcinogen-regulated area, is it done in a manner that will not contaminate non-regulated areas or the external environment?

TIRE INFLATION

☐ Where tires are mounted and/or inflated on drop center wheels or on wheels with split rims and/or retainer rings, is a safe practice procedure posted and enforced?

☐ Does each tire inflation hose have a clip-on chuck with at least 2.54 inches (6.45 centimeters) of hose between the chuck and an in-line hand valve and gauge?

☐ Does the tire inflation control valve automatically shut off the air flow when the valve is released?

☐ Is a tire restraining device such as a cage, rack, or other effective means used while inflating tires mounted on split rims or rims using retainer rings?

☐ Are employees prohibited from standing directly over or in front of a tire while it is being inflated?

OSHA Assistance

OSHA'S OFFICE OF SMALL BUSINESS ASSISTANCE

OSHA created the Office of Small Business Assistance to help small business employers understand their safety and health obligations, access compliance information, provide guidance in regulatory standards, and to educate them about cost-effective means for ensuring the safety and health of worksites.

OSHA's Office of Small Business Assistance can be contacted by telephone at (202) 693-2220 or by writing to the U.S. Department of Labor, 200 Constitution Avenue, NW, Room N-3700, Washington, DC 20210.

ON-SITE CONSULTATION

Using the free and confidential on-site consultation service largely funded by the Federal OSHA, employers can find out about potential hazards at their worksites, improve their occupational safety and health management systems, and even qualify for a one-year exemption from routine OSHA inspections.

The service is delivered at your workplace by state governments using well-trained professional staff. Most consultations take place on-site, though limited services away from the worksite are available.

Primarily targeted for smaller businesses, this safety and health Consultation Program is completely separate from OSHA's enforcement efforts. It is also confidential. No inspections are triggered by using the Consultation Program and no citations are issued or penalties proposed.

Your name, your firm's name and any information you provide about your workplace, plus any unsafe or unhealthful working conditions that the consultant uncovers, will not routinely be reported to the OSHA enforcement staff.

Your only obligation will be to commit to correcting serious job safety and health hazards discovered -- a commitment that you are expected to make prior to the actual consultation visit. If hazards are discovered, the consultant will work with you to ensure they are corrected in a reasonable timeframe agreed upon by all parties.

Getting Started. Since consultation is a voluntary activity, you must request it. Your telephone call or letter sets the consulting machinery in motion. The consultant will discuss your specific needs and set up a visit date based on the priority assigned to your request, your work schedule and the time needed for the consultant to prepare adequately to serve you. OSHA encourages a complete review of your firm's safety and health situation; however, if you wish, you may limit the visit to one or more specific problems.

Opening Conference. When the consultant arrives at your worksite for the scheduled visit, he or she will first meet with you in an opening conference to briefly review the consultant's role and the obligations you incur as an employer.

Walk-through. Together, you and the consultant will examine conditions in your workplace. OSHA strongly encourages maximum employee participation in the walk-through. Better informed and alert employees can help you identify and correct potential injury and illness hazards in your workplace. Talking with employees during the walk-through helps the consultant identify and judge the nature and extent of specific hazards.

The consultant will study your entire workplace, or only those specific operations you designate, and discuss applicable OSHA standards. The consultant also will point out other safety or health risks which might not be cited under OSHA standards, but which nevertheless may pose safety or health risks to your employees. He or she may suggest and even provide measures such as self-inspection and safety and health training that you and your employees can apply to prevent future hazardous situations.

A comprehensive consultation also includes: (1) appraisal of all mechanical and environmental hazards and physical work practices; (2) appraisal of the present job safety and health program or help in establishing one; (3) a conference with management on findings; (4) a written report of recommendations and agreements; and (5) training and assistance with implementing recommendations.

Closing Conference. The consultant will then review detailed findings with you in a closing conference. You will learn not only what you need to improve but what you are doing right, as well. At that time you can discuss problems, possible solutions and abatement periods to eliminate or control any serious hazards identified during the walk-through.

In rare instances, the consultant may find an "imminent danger" situation during the walk-through. In that case, you must take immediate action to protect employees. In certain other situations–those that would be judged a "serious violation" under OSHA criteria–you and the consultant must develop and agree to a reasonable plan and schedule to eliminate or control that hazard. The consultant will offer general approaches and options to you. He or she may also suggest other sources for technical help.

Abatement and Follow-through. Following the closing conference, the consultant will send you a detailed written report explaining the findings and confirming any abatement periods agreed upon. The consultant may also contact you from time to time to check your progress. You, of course, may always contact him or her for assistance.

Ultimately, OSHA does require hazard abatement so that each consultation visit achieves its objective–effective employee protection. If you fail to eliminate or control identified serious hazards (or an imminent danger) according to the plan and within the limits agreed upon or an agreed-upon extension, the situation must be referred from consultation to an OSHA enforcement office for appropriate action. This type of referral is *extremely* rare.

Benefits. Knowledge of your workplace hazards and ways to eliminate them can only improve your own operations–and the management of your firm. You will get professional advice and assistance on the correction of workplace hazards and benefit from on-site training and assistance provided. The consultant can help you establish or strengthen an employee safety and health program, making safety and health activities routine rather than crisis-oriented responses.

In many states, employers may participate in OSHA's Safety and Health Achievement Recognition Program (SHARP). This program is designed to provide incentives and support to smaller, high-hazard employers to develop, implement and continuously improve effective safety and health programs at their worksite(s). SHARP provides recognition of employers who have demonstrated exemplary achievements in workplace safety and health, beginning with a comprehensive safety and health consultation visit, correction of all workplace safety and health hazards, adoption and implementation of effective safety and health management systems, and agreement to request further consultative visits if major changes in working conditions or processes occur

that may introduce new hazards. Employers who meet these specific SHARP requirements may be removed from OSHA's programmed inspection list for one year.

The on-site consultants **will:**

- help you recognize hazards in your workplace,

- suggest general approaches or options for solving a safety or health problem,

- identify kinds of help available if you need further assistance,

- provide you with a written report summarizing findings,

- assist you in developing or maintaining an effective safety and health program,

- provide training and education for you and your employees,

- recommend you for a one-year exclusion from OSHA programmed inspections, once program criteria are met.

The on-site consultants **will not:**

- issue citations or propose penalties for violations of OSHA standards,

- report possible violations to OSHA enforcement staff,

- guarantee that your workplace will "pass" an OSHA inspection.

For a list of consultation projects in each state, see the OSHA website at www.osha.gov/dcsp/smallbusiness/consult_directory.html.

OTHER COOPERATIVE PROGRAMS

Information about OSHA's different cooperative programs is available from any OSHA Regional Office, OSHA Area Office, or by contacting OSHA's Directorate of Cooperative and State Programs at the U.S. Department of Labor, Occupational Safety and Health Administration, 200 Constitution Avenue, NW, Room N-3700, Washington, DC 20210, phone (202) 693-2200.

OSHA
Occupational Safety and
Health Administration

VOLUNTARY PROTECTION PROGRAMS (VPP)

OSHA's VPP provide an opportunity for labor, management and government to work together cooperatively to further the goal of providing effective safety and health protection in the workplace. The VPP grant recognition to worksites that provide or are committed to providing effective protection for their employees through implementation of systematically managed safety and health programs. The Star Program is for worksites that have at least one year's experience with an effectively implemented safety and health program. The Merit Program is for worksites working toward an effectively implemented program. The Star Demonstration Program is for worksites with programs at Star quality but with some aspect of their program that requires further study by OSHA. All participants work in partnership with OSHA and provide models for OSHA and for their industries.

OSHA STRATEGIC PARTNERSHIP PROGRAM (OSPP)

OSPP is designed to enable groups of employers, employees and employee representatives to partner with OSHA and enter into an extended, voluntary, cooperative relationship in order to encourage, assist and recognize efforts to eliminate serious hazards and achieve a high level of worker safety and health.

OSHA ALLIANCE PROGRAM

Alliances are goal-oriented written agreements between OSHA and organizations to work together to prevent workplace injuries and illnesses. Organizations include employers, employees, labor unions, trade or professional groups, educational institutions and government agencies. Alliances focus on one or more of the following goals: training and education, outreach and communications, and promoting the national dialogue on occupational safety and health.

States with Approved Plans

The *Occupational Safety and Health Act of 1970* encourages states to develop and operate their own job safety and health programs. OSHA approves and monitors state plans and provides up to 50 percent of an approved plan's operating costs.

Twenty-four states, Puerto Rico and the Virgin Islands currently operate approved state plans.

These state plans operate under authority of state law and are required to be, in structure and performance, "at least as effective as" the Federal OSHA Program. Although many states have adopted standards and procedures identical to Federal standards, states may have different or additional requirements parallel to those described in the Federal program.

To determine which set of standards and regulations apply to you, you need to know whether you are covered by a state plan or subject to Federal OSHA. Please visit http://www.oshaslc.gov/fso/osp/index.html, call the OSHA Area Office nearest you, or (800) 321-OSHA to obtain this information.

If you are subject to state enforcement, the OSHA Area Office will refer you to your state office which can provide all relevant information, such as whether the state is using the Federal standards, information on the poster and recordkeeping requirements, and special services available to small businesses. The state office also can provide you with further assistance, including directing you to the free, on-site consultation services described above.

See the list of OSHA-approved state plans at www.osha.gov.

OSHA Publications

A single free copy of the following materials can be obtained from the OSHA Area or Regional Office, or contact the OSHA Publications Office, U.S. Department of Labor, 200 Constitution Avenue, NW, N-3101, Washington, DC 20210, or call (202) 693-1888, or fax (202) 693-2498.

Access to Medical and Exposure Records – OSHA 3110

All About OSHA – OSHA 3302

Asbestos Standard for the Construction Industry – OSHA 3096

Control of Hazardous Energy (Lockout/Tagout) – OSHA 3120

Employee Workplace Rights – OSHA 3021

Employer Rights and Responsibilities Following an OSHA Inspection – OSHA 3000 (Spanish version 3195)

Hand and Power Tools – OSHA 3080

How to Plan for Workplace Emergencies and Evacuations – OSHA 3088

Job Safety and Health Protection Poster – OSHA 3165

Job Hazard Analysis – OSHA 3071

Model Plans & Programs for the OSHA Bloodborne Pathogens and Hazard Communications Standards – OSHA 3186

Occupational Safety and Health (OSH) Act – OSHA 2001

Personal Protective Equipment – OSHA 3151

Servicing Single-Piece and Multi-Piece Rim Wheels – OSHA 3086

The following publications are available from the U.S. Government Printing Office (GPO), Superintendent of Documents, Washington, DC 20402, phone toll-free (866) 512-1800, fax (202) 512-2250. Include GPO Order Number and make checks payable to Superintendent of Documents. All prices are subject to change by GPO.

Hazard Communication: A Compliance Kit – OSHA 3111
Order No. 029-016-00200-6. Cost: $21.00

Construction Industry Digest – OSHA 2202
Order No. 029-016-00212-0. Cost: $8.00

Materials Handling and Storing – OSHA 2236
Order No. 029-016-00215-4. Cost: $3.75

Internet—There is an enormous amount of compliance assistance information on OSHA's website that can be useful to the small business owner, found at http://www.osha.gov/dcsp/compliance_assistance/index.html. OSHA standards, interpretations, directives and additional information are also available at http://www.osha.gov/ and http://www.osha-slc.gov/.

CD-ROM—A wide variety of OSHA materials, including standards, interpretations, directives, and more, can be purchased on CD-ROM from the U.S. Government Printing Office, Superintendent of Documents, phone toll-free (866) 512-1800.

Emergencies—For life-threatening situations, call (800) 321-OSHA. Your call will be directed to the nearest OSHA Area or state office for help.

For further information on any OSHA program, contact your nearest OSHA Area or Regional Office or call (800) 321-OSHA.

Other Sources of Assistance

VOLUNTARY PROTECTION PROGRAMS PARTICIPANTS' ASSOCIATION (VPPPA)

The VPPPA is a private organization made up of VPP participant companies. The VPPPA has members in most states where the Federal OSHA program operates and in many states where state plans are in force. The VPPPA is willing to provide information, outreach, and mentoring to help worksites improve their safety and health programs. Chapters of the national association have been formed in most OSHA regions. Members of these chapters also are willing to provide the kind of assistance provided by the national organization. To contact your regional chapter of the VPPPA, call or write the OSHA Regional Office listed in the back of this publication for the address and telephone number of the chapter in your region. To contact the VPPPA national organization, please call (703) 761-1146 or write to the following address:

Voluntary Protection Programs Participants' Association
7600 East Leesburg Pike, Suite 440
Falls Church, VA 22043
(703) 761-1146

SMALL BUSINESS DEVELOPMENT CENTERS

The U.S. Small Business Administration (SBA) administers the Small Business Development Center Program to provide management and technical assistance to current and prospective small business owners. There is a Small Business Development Center (SBDC) in every state, the District of Columbia, Puerto Rico, Guam, Samoa, and the U.S. Virgin Islands, with more than 1,000 service centers across the country. SBDC assistance is tailored to the local community and the needs of individual clients and designed to deliver up-to-date counseling, training, and technical assistance. Services could include helping small businesses with financial, marketing, production, organization, engineering, and technical problems.

OSHA
Occupational Safety and
Health Administration

NATIONAL INSTITUTE FOR OCCUPATIONAL SAFETY AND HEALTH (NIOSH)

NIOSH is a research agency in the U.S. Department of Health and Human Services. (OSHA is a regulatory agency in the U.S. Department of Labor). NIOSH conducts research and makes recommendations to prevent work-related illness and injury. NIOSH has produced a useful guide, *Safety and Health Resource Guide for Small Businesses*, with telephone numbers, e-mail and Internet addresses, and mailing information to enable small businesses to contact government agencies, private organizations, consultants, and others who can help with occupational safety and health issues. The NIOSH toll-free phone number is (800) 356-4674, and its website address is www.cdc.gov/niosh.

WORKERS' COMPENSATION CARRIERS AND OTHER INSURANCE COMPANIES

Many workers' compensation carriers, as well as many liability and fire insurance companies, conduct periodic inspections and visits to evaluate safety and health hazards. Managers of small and medium-sized businesses need to know what services are available from these sources. Contact your carrier and see what it has to offer.

TRADE ASSOCIATIONS AND EMPLOYER GROUPS

Because of the increase in job safety and health awareness resulting from OSHA activities, many trade associations and employer groups have put a new emphasis on safety and health matters to better serve their members. If you are a member of such a group, find out how it is assisting its members. If you are not a member, find out if these groups are circulating their materials to nonmembers, as many do.

TRADE UNIONS AND EMPLOYEE GROUPS

If your employees are organized, set up some communications, as you do in normal labor relations, to get coordinated action on hazards in your business. Safety and health is one area where advance planning will produce action on common goals. Many trade unions have safety and health expertise that they are willing to share.

THE NATIONAL SAFETY COUNCIL AND LOCAL CHAPTERS

The National Safety Council (NSC) has a broad range of information services available. If you have a local chapter of the NSC in your area, you can call or visit to see how you can use materials pertaining to your business. If there is no chapter nearby, you can write to:

National Safety Council
1121 Spring Lake Drive
Itasca, IL 60143-3201

PROFESSIONAL ASSOCIATIONS

The following professional associations are an additional resource that may be able to provide assistance to you:

American Society of Safety Engineers
1800 East Oakton Street
Des Plaines, IL 60018-2187

American Industrial Hygiene Association
2700 Prosperity Avenue
Suite 250
Fairfax, VA 22031-4319

American Conference of Governmental
Industrial Hygienists
1330 Kemper Meadow Drive
Cincinnati, OH 45240

SPECIFIC MEDICAL CONSULTATION

Talk to your local doctors or clinics for advice on workplace medical matters on a consulting basis. Contact your local Red Cross chapter for assistance in first-aid training. If you cannot identify a local chapter, call (800) 667-2968 or write to:

American National Red Cross
National Headquarters
Safety Programs
2025 E Street, NW
Washington, DC 20006

YOUR LOCAL LIBRARY

Many local or university libraries contain information on specific safety and health subjects pertaining to your business. These materials are usually in reference rooms or technical subject areas. Ask your librarian what is available. The library may be able to obtain materials for you through inter-library loan, purchase, etc.

Two basic publications of the National Safety Council will give you many sources of technical information. The *Accident Prevention Manual for Industrial Operations* is a basic reference book for all safety and health work. The second book, *Fundamentals of Industrial Hygiene*, contains excellent information on toxic materials and recommended health and hygiene practices. Both of these references list other sources at the end of each chapter that may help you in solving specific problems.

FINANCING WORKPLACE IMPROVEMENT

The SBA is authorized to make loans to assist small businesses with meeting OSHA standards. Because SBA's definition of a "small" business varies from industry to industry, contact your local SBA field office to determine whether you qualify.

A helpful hint: if you decide to apply for an SBA loan, experience indicates that most delays in processing SBA/OSHA loans are because applications (1) do not adequately describe each workplace condition to be corrected and identify one or more OSHA standards applicable to the condition to be corrected, or (2) do not provide a reasonable estimate of the cost to correct each condition.

In most cases, safety hazards can be corrected without financial assistance. Health hazards may be more costly to correct. The age and condition of the building and equipment are major factors to be considered.

Interest rate information on SBA loans may be obtained from any SBA office. They fluctuate but are generally lower than you can obtain elsewhere. You may wish to consult your own bank. It pays to shop around for loans.

Don't forget to check with your accountant at income tax time, since safety and health improvements can often be expensed or depreciated.

ADDITIONAL WEB PAGES OF INTEREST TO SMALL BUSINESSES

(Internet websites change frequently; these listings may not be current.)

http://www.firstgov.gov
A website for all agencies of the Federal government.

http://www.sba.gov
The U.S. Small Business Administration's home page.

http://www.businesslaw.gov
Legal and regulatory information for small businesses by state.

http://www.regulations.gov
A site to enable small business owners to find all Federal regulations that are open for comment, to read them and to submit their views.

http://www.assistancecenters.net/
For help with understanding environmental regulations that relate to the operation of your business.

http://www.irs.gov/businesses/small/index.html
This Internal Revenue Service website offers industry- and profession-specific tax information and guidelines.

Major Action Steps to be Taken	Priority (Assign each Step a Number)	Projected Completion Date	Actual Completion Date
1. _____ _____ _____	_____	_____	_____
2. _____ _____ _____	_____	_____	_____
3. _____ _____ _____	_____	_____	_____
4. _____ _____ _____	_____	_____	_____
5. _____ _____ _____	_____	_____	_____
6. _____ _____ _____	_____	_____	_____
7. _____ _____ _____	_____	_____	_____
8. _____ _____ _____	_____	_____	_____
9. _____ _____ _____	_____	_____	_____
10. _____ _____ _____	_____	_____	_____

Description of Action to be Taken: _____

_____

_____

Specific Steps Required	Persons Assigned	Projected Completion Date	Problems/ Delays Encountered	Actual Completion Date
1. _____ _____ _____ _____ _____ _____	_____	_____	_____	_____
2. _____ _____ _____ _____ _____ _____	_____	_____	_____	_____
3. _____ _____ _____ _____ _____ _____	_____	_____	_____	_____
4. _____ _____ _____ _____ _____	_____	_____	_____	_____
5. _____ _____ _____ _____ _____	_____	_____	_____	_____

OSHA
Occupational Safety and Health Administration

The following statements provide examples that can be used or modified by employers to help prevent employee injury and illness.

"The Occupational Safety and Health Act of 1970 clearly states our common goal of safe and healthful working conditions. The safety and health of our employees continues to be the first consideration in the operation of this business. "

"Safety and health in our business must be a part of every operation. Without question it is every employee's responsibility at all levels. "

"It is the intent of this company to comply with all laws. To do this we must constantly be aware of conditions in all work areas that can produce injuries. No employee is required to work at a job he or she knows is not safe or healthful. Your cooperation in detecting hazards and, in turn, controlling them is a condition of your employment. Inform your supervisor immediately of any situation beyond your ability or authority to correct. "

"The personal safety and health of each employee of this company is of primary importance. The prevention of occupationally-induced injuries and illnesses is of such consequence that it will be given precedence over operating productivity whenever necessary. To the greatest degree possible, management will provide all mechanical and physical facilities required for personal safety and health in keeping with the highest standards. "

"We will maintain a safety and health program conforming to the best practices of organizations of this type. To be successful, such a program must embody the proper attitudes toward injury and illness prevention on the part of supervisors and employees. It also requires cooperation in all safety and health matters, not only between supervisor and employee, but also between each employee and his or her co-workers. Only through such a cooperative effort can a safety program in the best interest of all be established and preserved. "

"Our objective is a safety and health program that will reduce the number of injuries and illnesses to an absolute minimum, not merely in keeping with, but surpassing, the best experience of operations similar to ours. Our goal is zero accidents and injuries. "

"Our safety and health program will include:

- Providing mechanical and physical safeguards to the maximum extent possible.

- A program of safety and health inspections to identify and eliminate unsafe working conditions or practices, to control health hazards, and to comply fully with the safety and health standards for every job.

- Training all employees in good safety and health practices.

- Providing necessary personal protective equipment and instructions for its use and care.

- Developing and enforcing safety and health rules and requiring that employees cooperate with these rules as a condition of employment.

- Investigating, promptly and thoroughly, every accident to find out what caused it and to correct the problem so that it won't happen again.

- Setting up a system of recognition and awards for outstanding safety service or performance. "

"We recognize that the responsibilities for safety and health are shared:

- The employer accepts responsibility for leadership of the safety and health program, for its effectiveness and improvement, and for providing safe conditions.

- Supervisors are responsible for developing the proper attitudes toward safety and health in themselves and in those they supervise, and for ensuring that all operations are performed with the utmost regard for the safety and health of all personnel involved, including themselves.

- Employees are responsible for compliance with all rules and regulations and for continuously practicing safety while performing their duties. "

This is a suggested code. It is general in nature and includes many types of small business activities. It is intended only as a model that you can customize to describe your own work environment.

General Policy

1. All employees of this firm shall follow these safe practice rules, render every possible aid to safe operations, and report all unsafe conditions or practices to the supervisor/employer.

2. Supervisors shall insist that employees observe and obey every rule, regulation, and order necessary to the safe conduct of the work and take such action necessary to obtain compliance.

3. All employees shall be given frequent accident prevention instructions. Instructions, practice drills, and articles concerning workplace safety and health shall be given at least once every _____ working days.

4. Anyone known to be under the influence of alcohol and/or drugs shall not be allowed on the job while in that condition. Persons with symptoms of alcohol and/or drug abuse are encouraged to discuss personal or work-related problems with the supervisor/employer.

5. No one shall knowingly be permitted or required to work while his or her ability or alertness is impaired by fatigue, illness, or other causes that might expose the individual or others to injury.

6. Employees should be alert to see that all guards and other protective devices are in proper places and adjusted, and they shall report deficiencies. Approved protective equipment shall be worn in specified work areas.

7. Horseplay, scuffling, and other acts that tend to endanger the safety or well-being of employees are prohibited.

8. Work shall be well planned and supervised to prevent injuries when working with equipment and handling heavy materials. When lifting heavy objects, employees should bend their knees and use the large muscles of the legs instead of the smaller muscles of the back. Back injuries are the most frequent and often the most persistent and painful type of workplace injury.

9. Workers shall not handle or tamper with any electrical equipment, machinery, or air or water lines in a manner not within the scope of their duties, unless they have received instructions from their supervisor/employer.

10. All injuries shall be reported promptly to the supervisor/employer so that arrangements can be made for medical and/or first-aid treatment. First-aid materials are located in _____; emergency, fire, ambulance, rescue squad, and doctors' telephone numbers are located _____; and fire extinguishers are located at _____.

Suggested Safety Rules

- Do not throw material, tools, or other objects from heights (whether structures or buildings) until proper precautions are taken to protect others from the falling object hazard.

- Wash thoroughly after handling injurious or poisonous substances.

- Gasoline shall not be used for cleaning purposes.

- When using a ladder, always face the steps and use both hands while climbing.

Use of Tools and Equipment

- Keep faces of hammers in good condition to avoid flying nails and bruised fingers.

- Files shall be equipped with handles; never use a file as a punch or pry.

- Do not use a screwdriver as a chisel.

- Do not lift or lower portable electric tools by the power cords; use a rope.

- Do not leave the cords of tools where cars or trucks will run over them.

Machinery and Vehicles

- Do not attempt to operate machinery or equipment without special permission unless it is part of your regular duties.

- Loose or frayed clothing, dangling ties, finger rings, etc., must not be worn around moving machinery or other places where they can get caught.

- Machinery shall not be repaired or adjusted while in operation.

OSHA has four separate sets of standards: General Industry (29 Code of Federal Regulations [CFR] 1910), Construction (29 CFR 1926), Maritime Employment (29 CFR 1915-1919), and Agriculture (29 CFR 1928). OSHA has regulations on posting and other administrative matters in 29 CFR 1903 and on recording and reporting of injuries and illnesses in 29 CFR 1904.

The OSH Act also has a general duty clause, section 5(a)(1), 29 U.S.C. 654(b)(1), which provides that:

(a) Each employer – –

(1) shall furnish to each of his employees employment and a place of employment which are free from recognized hazards that are causing or are likely to cause death or serious physical harm to his employees.

A recognized hazard is a danger recognized by the employer's industry or industry in general, by the employer, or by common sense. The general duty clause does not apply if there is an OSHA standard dealing with the hazard, unless the employer knows that the standard does not adequately address the hazard.

General Industry, Maritime, and Construction OSHA standards are available at www.osha.gov.

After you have obtained a copy of the current standards, identify those that apply to your business by a process of elimination. Read the introduction to the subpart heading, and then analyze the possible hazards in terms of **your** workplace, **your** equipment, **your** materials and of **your** employees. For example, if you are engaged in retail trade or service and you do not have compressed gases, flammables, or explosives on your premises, you can eliminate Hazardous Materials (Subpart H) as not applying to your business.

If you have any questions in determining whether a standard is applicable to your workplace, you may contact the nearest OSHA Area Office for assistance. Staff there should be able to answer any questions you may have about standards and provide general guidelines on methods of implementation in your workplace. Small businesses are encouraged to participate in the development of standards.

In 1996, Congress passed the Small Business Regulatory Enforcement Fairness Act, or SBREFA, in response to concerns expressed by the small business community that Federal regulations were too numerous, too complex and too expensive to implement. SBREFA was designed to give small businesses assistance in understanding and complying with regulations and more of a voice in the development of new regulations. Under SBREFA, the Occupational Safety and Health Administration (OSHA) and other Federal agencies must:

- Produce Small Entity Compliance Guides for some rules;

- Be responsive to small business inquiries about compliance with the agency's regulations;

- Submit final rules to Congress for review;

- Have a penalty reduction policy for small businesses; and

- Involve small businesses in the development of some proposed rules through Small Business Advocacy Review Panels.

Commenting on Enforcement Actions

Under a law passed by Congress in 1996, the Small Business Administration (SBA) has established an SBA Ombudsman and SBA Regional Fairness Boards to investigate small business complaints about Federal agency enforcement actions. If you are a small business and believe that you have been treated unfairly by OSHA, you may file an electronic comment/complaint with the SBA Ombudsman over the Internet at: http://www.sba.gov/ombudsman/comments/commentform1.html Or you may contact the SBA's Office of the National Ombudsman by:

- Toll-Free Phone: (888) REG-FAIR (734-3247)

- Fax: (202) 481-5719

- E-mail: ombudsman@sba.gov

- Mail: Office of the National Ombudsman U.S. Small Business Administration 409 3rd Street, S.W., MC2120 Washington, DC 20416-0005

To view the SBREFA Act in its entirety, please visit the following web link: http://www.sba.gov/advo/laws/sbrefa.html

For more information on SBREFA the following web links may prove helpful: http://www.sba.gov/ombudsman/ http://www.sba.gov/ombudsman/dsp_overview.html http://www.sba.gov/ombudsman/dsp_faq.html http://www.sba.gov/advo/ http://www.sba.gov/advo/laws/is_oshapanel.html

NOTE: Filing a complaint with the SBA Ombudsman does not affect any obligation that you may have to comply with an OSHA citation or other enforcement action. Nor does it mean that you need not take other available legal steps to protect your interests.

OSHA Regional Offices

Region I
(CT,* ME, MA, NH, RI, VT*)
JFK Federal Building, Room E340
Boston, MA 02203
(617) 565-9860

Region II
(NJ,* NY,* PR,* VI*)
201 Varick Street, Room 670
New York, NY 10014
(212) 337-2378

Region III
(DE, DC, MD,* PA, VA,* WV)
The Curtis Center
170 S. Independence Mall West
Suite 740 West
Philadelphia, PA 19106-3309
(215) 861-4900

Region IV
(AL, FL, GA, KY,* MS, NC,* SC,* TN*)
61 Forsyth Street, SW, Room 6T50
Atlanta, GA 30303
(404) 562-2300

Region V
(IL, IN,* MI,* MN,* OH, WI)
230 South Dearborn Street
Room 3244
Chicago, IL 60604
(312) 353-2220

Region VI
(AR, LA, NM,* OK, TX)
525 Griffin Street, Room 602
Dallas, TX 75202
(972) 850-4145

Region VII
(IA,* KS, MO, NE)
Two Pershing Square
2300 Main Street, Suite 1010
Kansas City, MO 64108-2416
(816) 283-8745

Region VIII
(CO, MT, NO, SO, UT,* WY*)
1999 Broadway, Suite 1690
PO Box 46550
Denver, CO 80202-5716
(720) 264-6550

Region IX
(American Samoa, AZ,* CA,* HI,* NV,* and Guam,
the Northern Mariana Islands and American
Samoa)
90 7th Street, Suite 18-100
San Francisco, CA 94103
(415) 625-2547

Region X
(AK,* ID, OR,* WA*)
1111 Third Avenue, Suite 715
Seattle, WA 98101-3212
(206) 553-5930

* These states and territories operate their own OSHA-approved job safety and health programs and cover state and local government employees as well as private sector employees. The Connecticut, New Jersey, New York and Virgin Islands plans cover public employees only. States with approved programs must have standards that are identical to, or at least as effective as, the Federal OSHA standards.

Note: To get contact information for OSHA Area Offices, OSHA-approved State Plans and OSHA Consultation Projects, please visit us online at www.osha.gov or call us at 1-800-321-0SHA.

Contact Information

The most complete and current information and e-mail addresses for OSHA Regional and Area Offices and the state Consultation Projects can be found on OSHA's website at www.osha.gov/html/oshdir.html or by contacting:

U.S. Department of Labor
Occupational Safety and Health Administration
Directorate of Cooperative and State Programs
Office of Small Business Assistance
200 Constitution Ave., NW
Washington, DC 20210
(800) 321-OSHA

OSHA's Non-Retaliation Policy

The Occupational Safety and Health Administration (OSHA) has a long-established policy that information inquiries received by the agency regarding safety and health regulations or other safety-related subjects shall **not** trigger an inspection. This policy is outlined in *OSHA Instruction CPL 02-00-103 (CPL 2.103), Field Inspection Reference Manual*, Section 5 - Chapter I, B.4.b. The exact wording is:

__Employer Contacts.__ Contacts for information initiated by employers or their representatives shall not trigger an inspection, nor shall such employer inquiries protect them against regular inspections conducted pursuant to guidelines established by the agency. Further, if an employer or its representatives indicates that an imminent danger exists or that a fatality or catastrophe has occurred, the Area Director shall act in accordance with established inspection priority procedures.

While exceptions to this policy exist, such as the presence of an imminent danger or the occurrence of a fatality, OSHA policy is to provide assistance to help employers prevent and reduce workplace fatalities, illnesses and injuries.

**Occupational Safety
and Health Administration**

U.S. Department of Labor

www.osha.gov